31 DAY CHALLENGE

A ONE-MONTH BATTLE PLAN TO WIN THE WAR AGAINST PORN

MATT MIZELL

Published in Carlsbad, California, by Mizell Publishing. Mizell Publishing and the coat of arms logo are protected by copyright.

Available from Amazon.com and other retail outlets. For bulk orders or more information, email matt@mattmizell.com or visit 31challenge.com.

ISBN-13: 978-1981104604 ISBN-10: 1981104607

"This book is practical, challenging, and honest about a taboo subject. It's a must read for anybody stuck in the cycle of shame and sexual sin."
   — CHASE FEINDEL, Lead Pastor, Anthem Church

"Many books explain the problem and psychology of a porn addiction, but this book gives hope through tangible and doable steps to break the addiction. This is a very powerful resource not only for men who have lived in shame for decades, but for youth struggling with lust, masturbation, and porn!"
   — SHEA CULLEN, Youth Pastor, Daybreak Church

"This amazing resource will change the scope of your struggle. Porn is barely scratching the surface; this book goes deep for healing."
   — REV. JEFF BRADY, Assistant Pastor, Hanfield UMC

"This book is a great tool to push you towards a life of moral integrity. Don't fight this battle alone. The addiction of sexual sin is the only addiction that can be fed through your own thoughts. Starve your brain of that endorphin cookie and your brain will crave it less and less."
   — CHAD GOTHMANN, Youth Minister, Sunrise Church of Christ

"In a culture saturated with opportunities to use porn, this resource creates the opportunity for real youth to find real victory. I am so grateful this resource exists."
   — ERIC WEST, Associate Pastor to Youth & Families, Gateway Baptist Church

"This book is much needed for our teenage guys, and for a lot of adult men who are struggling with pornography, masturbation, and sexual addiction. It is a struggle that we often battle alone, and using this resource as the basis for accountability with brothers in Christ will be a great offense in this war we are fighting against this and ALL of the addictions that we face."
   — REV. JOE PALMER, Pastor with Families & Students, Trinity UMC

"Drink deeply and desperately from the flowing stream of God's infinite grace. Be satisfied with Jesus and forbidden water will lose its taste."
   — STEPHEN BALLARD, Youth Minister, East Union Baptist Church

"This book is a powerful resource for everyone fighting the battle of our generation against the onslaught of unhealthy imagery, pre-marital self-gratification and shame."
— SCOTT STRATCHAN, High School & Young Adult Minister, Faith Lutheran Church

"I believe God will use this book to change your life forever. Though your efforts may fail, Jesus' commitment to you never will. I dealt with a 10-year pornography addiction and He brought me through it. He will bring you through it."
— COLTON WHEELER, Children's & Youth Pastor, First Baptist Church Lakeside City

"The 31 Day Challenge literally gives you the tools to live a life of faithfulness and purity. This book is the shot in the arm so many of us men need to get. When it comes to the quest for sexual integrity, Matt helped me see that you can live a life fully devoted to Christ. Praying for you and your journey."
— ADAM KUNTZ, Student Pastor, Living Stones Church

"A challenging read for all walks of life and all ages, due to the access all of us have to this material. This content is necessary for all to absorb, understand and fully appreciate as we continue to increase God's Kingdom."
— JEFF MYERS

"A goal cannot be achieved without an understanding of the 'why' behind the goal and having specific tactics to implement. The book provides both and thus will lead you to freedom."
— RYAN GREENWALD

"Stop giving your bride—present or future—competition. She shouldn't have to live up to the lies of porn."
— STEVEN MURPHY

"A day-by-day guide for gaining victory over your hidden sin and a useful tool for gaining a healthy perspective on how your sin affects you and those around you."
— KEENAN KLAMER

*Dedicated to guys sick of losing
the war that's ruining their life.*

CONTENTS

ix	Consider the Cost
xxi	Challenge Accepted?
xxiii	Personalize Your Battle Plan
xxx	Go Streaking
1	Day 1 — Face Your Enemy
9	Day 2 — Submit To God
13	Day 3 — Nobody's Perfect
19	Day 4 — You Aren't Alone
23	Day 5 — Father of Lies
27	Day 6 — Word of Caution
33	Day 7 — Greater Is He
37	Day 8 — More Than Conquerors
41	Day 9 — Flee From This
47	Day 10 — Feel Alive
53	Day 11 — By No Means
57	Day 12 — Unconditional Forgiveness
61	Day 13 — Do Not Enter
67	Day 14 — Keep Watching
71	Day 15 — Your Secret Weapon
77	Day 16 — Draw Near

81	Day 17 — Your Way Out
85	Day 18 — Oh So Sweet
89	Day 19 — Master Over You
93	Day 20 — Make the Promise
97	Day 21 — Smooth Talk
103	Day 22 — This Great Evil
107	Day 23 — Extreme Measures
113	Day 24 — Display Strength
117	Day 25 — Make Up Your Mind
121	Day 26 — Innocent Blood
125	Day 27 — Consistently Honorable
129	Day 28 — Consider It Pure Joy
135	Day 29 — Be On Guard
139	Day 30 — Abstain From Evil
143	Day 31 — Hide the Word
151	Tough Questions
153	Action Steps Overview
155	Dear Sex Trafficking Victim…
157	Dear Sex Trafficker…
159	About the Author
161	Acknowledgements
163	Notes

CONSIDER THE COST

You're in a war.

And you're fighting a new battle every single day.

Let's stop tiptoeing around the too-private-to-talk-about subject of PMO and throw down with this issue face-to-face.

What's PMO? To the average teenager, it stands for "pissing me off", but according to the Urban Dictionary[1], PMO stands for porn, masturbation and non-marital orgasm.

In short—PMO is pretty much any sexual sin.

When it comes to your war against PMO, here's the bottom line:

You're losing.

Losing *what* exactly?

For one, you're losing daily battles by giving into temptation. But you're losing much more than that.

You're losing perspective. Losing trust. Losing integrity. Losing self-control. Losing intimacy. Losing yourself. You're just losing.

If you're married, you're losing closeness with your spouse. It doesn't matter how often you do or don't have sex—intimacy is draining every time you give in to PMO.

If you're single, you're robbing yourself from intimacy with the person you'll end up with one day.

You have to stop. You must stop. You have no other option.

In 2017, Time magazine announced its Person of the Year award would actually go to a group of people rather than an individual.

The group of people? The Silence Breakers[2].

The Silence Breakers refer to the women who came forward, ultimately in droves, to speak up about sexual misconduct by powerful men.

What initially started as accusations against Hollywood film producer Harvey Weinstein turned into a flood of accusations against dozens of well-known celebrities, business owners, and politicians.

Guys who were once household names[3]—like NFL Hall of Famer Marshall Faulk, NBC "Today" news anchor Matt Lauer, Emmy-winning actor and comedian Louis C.K., actor Steven Seagal, actor Dustin Hoffman, Senator Al Franken, television host and journalist Charlie Rose, Chief White House political correspondent for the New York Times Glenn Thrush, hip hop producer Russell Simmons, CW producer Andrew Kreisberg, Republican Senate nominee Roy

Moore, NPR news chief Michael Oreskes, celebrity chef Mario Batali, Boston Symphony Orchestra music director James Levine, USA Gymnastics doctor Larry Nasser, Hollywood writer and director James Toback, actor and comedian Bill Cosby, actor Kevin Spacey, Pastor Ted Haggard and Pastor Matthew Tague—all not only lost their jobs, contracts or income, but most forfeited their entire careers due to their alleged lack of self-control.

This isn't even to mention their destroyed marriages, shattered respect from kids and colleagues, and trashed legacies.

Perhaps not all of these men were addicted to porn, but the common denominator in every one of their stories was a demonstrated lack of self-control that led to a pattern of sexual misconduct.

If you have the ego, pride or audacity to simply assume you can just go on doing the same things you've been doing and just hope that, magically, one day, things will just somehow be better—they won't.

Sexual sin is more captivating and powerful than even some of the most powerful men in the world—or should I say formerly-most-powerful men in the world—would like to admit.

It's nice to think that your little addiction isn't hurting anyone, but you're only kidding yourself.

Most people with whom I've spoken are either naïve or oblivious to the fact that sex trafficking is a major contributor to the porn industry in the United States.

What exactly is sex trafficking?

Sex trafficking[4] is a modern-day form of slavery in which a commercial sex act is induced by force, fraud, or coercion. If the victim is under the age of 18, *any* commercialized act of sex is considered sex trafficking regardless of force, fraud or coercion.

Porn fuels the sex trafficking industry.

In 2000, the Trafficking Victims Protection Act[5] (TVPA) made sex trafficking a violation of Federal law punishable by up to 20 years in prison per violation. Yet in 2014, the sex trafficking industry still generated an estimated $975 million in revenue in just eight cities in the United States[6].

According to a 2015 report[7], 63% of survivors of sex trafficking indicated that porn was made of them during their exploitation. There is no doubt that porn production is a major driving force behind the sex trafficking industry.

The average age for recruitment for sex trafficking[8] is 12-14 years old, while victimization typically ranges from 12-22.

In nearly every major middle and high school throughout the country, teenagers are being pursued, targeted and coerced into an industry that can undoubtedly ruin their lives.

As a father of a daughter, I am horrified to think of so many little girls being lured, forced or otherwise coerced to be part of such a sickening industry.

What's this got to do with you?

Supply is based on demand.

If you have convinced yourself that your addiction to pornography is not currently hurting someone else, you can't be any further from the truth!

Fathers are losing daughters, brothers are losing sisters, sisters are losing brothers, and lives are being destroyed… partly due to your habit "that isn't hurting anyone."

This isn't even to mention the harm and destruction you are causing yourself. Your choices are resulting in unspeakable damage to yourself each time you give in to sexual sin.

This is why Paul said[9]:

"All other sins a person commits are outside the body, but whoever sins sexually, sins against their own body."

You're messing up your own future by continuing to allow the cancer of porn invade your mind and body.

What makes things even worse is the tempting nature of the porn industry is getting even more powerful.

In 2016, the video game Pokémon Go was released, enabling players to use smart phone cameras to find monsters in real world locations.

Adoption of the game went viral, and millions of players went out in droves to parks, malls, schools and anywhere else they could possibly detect a monster.

This was the first video game to blend reality with digital overlaid images, creating a new segment of virtual reality that was coined "augmented reality."

Less than one year later, Apple announced in the Worldwide Developers Conference its launch of ARKit, allowing developers to create advanced augmented reality apps for iOS devices.

Augmented reality will likely provide a lot of exciting and helpful ways to engage in our world in ways we've never experienced it before. Driving may become easier than ever with augmented reality turn-by-turn navigation that includes holographs overlaid on streets. Cooks may become better in the kitchen with displays showing exactly how much of an ingredient to add to a pan. Surgeons may save more lives with screens that show them exactly where cancerous cells need to be removed.

Augmented reality is going to become more prevalent than ever before, and the technology will likely work its way into nearly every area of our lives.

While there are definitely positive benefits to augmented reality, we are about to exposed to a segment of the porn industry that will make a sexual experience more realistic than ever before.

I don't think we're too far away from reading news articles stating that Paris Hilton or other Playboy girls have signed deals with content creators to deliver lifelike augmented reality sexual experiences that can be digitally delivered to bedrooms around the world.

Each time technology advances, so do the temptations. With temptations becoming more and more powerful, it's foolish to think that your habits will dissipate and go away on their own.

Things aren't going to change on their own—unless you're willing to make some serious changes.

Damage may already be done, and while some of that damage may not be reversible, you can at least stop from causing more.

How?

You might have lost hundreds of battles over the years, but the war isn't over.

While ultimately you *need* to win the war against PMO, you likely won't win in a day.

Yet, by making small tweaks and changes in the days to come, where you find yourself in 31 days from now may surprise you.

You might be so deep into PMO that you can't imagine life without it. You want a life without it, but you don't think it's possible.

It *is* possible.

Let's go to war. Let's win some battles together. It's time to start fighting like you actually mean it.

You've been attempting to satisfy a legitimate desire in an illegitimate way.

The desire you've been trying to satisfy may not even relate to your sexual appetite. Your may have a desire for more companionship. Maybe you have a desire to be noticed. Maybe it's a desire to feel valued. Maybe it's something else altogether.

It may be necessary to uncover past wounds inflicted by others. Maybe you have faced abuse. Maybe you've been rejected. Maybe you feel like you're not in control.

Maybe you're oftentimes just bored with nothing else going on and that's when you find yourself getting into trouble.

Maybe the guys you hang out with aren't living that great of a lifestyle, and you find yourself going with the flow for how they live their lives, even though you want something different for your own.

For many guys, their addiction to PMO isn't based on their sexual appetite. Their addiction is a mere symptom of something else unhealthy in their life.

Whether there's something lacking in your life or you have a strong desire for sex, you simply cannot justify your addiction to PMO.

Let's face it—whatever you've tried so far to eliminate this problem from your life simply hasn't worked. Otherwise, you likely wouldn't be reading this right now.

This guide gives you a day-by-day battle plan. That's what you need. Something to help you get through one day at a time.

We've all heard about the studies that claim it takes 21 days to *create* a new habit. In this case, our goal is to *break* an old habit in 21 days.

Newer research[10] shows, however, that it may take longer than 21 days, and that habits are actually solidified or destroyed between 30 and 66 days.

Therefore, for the next 31 days, your goal is to completely rid yourself from your addiction to porn, masturbation and non-marital orgasms.

Of course you're welcome to make it your personal goal to refrain for 66 days. After all, the goal isn't to just get to 31 days and then go back to your old ways. The hope is that after 31 days, your old, destructive habits will be broken and you will have created new, healthy habits along the way.

As crazy as it sounds, you've gotta go cold turkey. If you allow yourself to screw up and have do-overs or mulligans along the way, you'll take them.

In addition, there are psychological milestones along the way, so it's really important that you don't adopt a weaning off mentality (no pun intended).

That being said, give yourself grace. If you relapse and make a mistake, don't start over. Celebrate how long you made your streak, dust yourself off, and pick up where you left off.

There's no need to start all over because the goal each day is the same.

Here's your goal each day: **win today's battle.**

Winning today's battle means you don't allow yourself to look at any porn whatsoever today. This includes videos, images, hard porn, soft porn, sexts, virtual reality, augmented reality… you name it.

Winning today's battle means you don't allow yourself to masturbate or engage in any other sexual sin that would lead you to orgasm unless your consenting spouse is involved.

You *can* do this. The cost of not doing this is far too great. You must accept this challenge.

CHALLENGE ACCEPTED?

This 31 Day Challenge is not only designed to help you break your PMO habit, but is intended to be a competition.

One of the greatest motivators known to mankind is competition.

Your war against PMO won't be won in just one day. This war will be won one battle at a time. Every day is a new battle.

Here's the competition: win 31 days in a row.

Are you capable of winning 31 battles in a row? Are you strong enough? Are you courageous enough? Are you sick and tired enough? Are you man enough?

Should you choose to take on this challenge, you will begin to win daily battles. As you begin to win daily battles, you will gain confidence and momentum that will fuel your desire and potential for victory in your battle. And then your next battle. And then your next.

There's a snowball effect, and the more wins you get, the easier conquering your addiction will become.

I was able to quit my addiction to porn by going cold turkey using the same methods I'm sharing with you now.

It is possible. You can do it. It has been done.

And victory in this area is far sweeter than I can describe in words.

No more shame. No more regret. No more feeling as though you're living a double life.

You can do this. You *must* do this.

For the 30 million victims[7] currently being exploited in the sex trafficking industry… take the challenge.

For the family members who have lost loved ones to this life-destroying industry… take the challenge.

For yourself, please… take the challenge.

While the challenge is to win 31 daily battles in a row in order to break your old habit, you're gonna accomplish it by taking on small chunks at a time.

Remember, your daily goal is this: **win today's battle.**

Don't worry about tomorrow. Don't think about the entire 31 days. Just focus on today. Each day in this guide is designed to help you win today's battle.

With multiple battles won, before you know it, you'll be winning the war, and you'll have completed the challenge.

Are you ready for it?

If so, it's time to personalize your battle plan.

PERSONALIZE YOUR BATTLE PLAN

If you want to defeat your enemy in a battle, what's your first step?

Do you rush right onto the battlefield with nothing more than just *hope* that you win?

No—not unless you're a foolish fighter.

You must first prepare.

Study your enemy to learn how they work. If you have a true desire to win, you cannot blindly meander into battle.

In the famous David v. Goliath showdown[11], it may appear that the little shepherd boy walked to the battlefield one day, saw Goliath taunting his older brothers and their army, and figured, "Why not? I've got nothing to lose. I'll head out with no preparation and fight this behemoth."

However, that simply wasn't the case. David had been training for quite a long time. He may not have known exactly what his future giant enemy would look like, but he had already been practicing by protecting his sheep from various enemies like lions, tigers and bears. Okay, maybe not the tigers, but you get the point. Each time he faced a smaller enemy, he stepped up to the challenge, fought hard and experienced a small victory.

When David finally came face-to-face with a bigger and stronger enemy, he was prepared.

How have you prepared for your war against PMO?

Maybe the better question is: Have you prepared at all?

Porn is an enemy that will destroy everything in your life if you don't get it under control and eliminate it altogether from your life.

You must prepare for battle. I'm pleading with you to take this war seriously. Too much is at stake if you don't.

In order to make this battle plan work best for you, it needs to be customized for who you are.

Here are five tactics to personalize your battle plan:

1. PREPARE EARLY

This guide is not intended to be read in one sitting. It's all about creating new habits that flush out the old. It's less about gaining the knowledge written in the pages of this book and more about suiting up for battle every day.

Take one day at a time. Set an alarm to go through each day the first thing in the morning. Temptations will be flung at you from all different directions throughout your day, but if you prepare early in the morning, you'll be ready to fight as you face your day.

2. TURN YOUR PHONE INTO A WEAPON

Fuel your daily battle plan by downloading helpful apps that turn your phone into a weapon. Some apps help create barriers to help prevent you from accessing porn, whereas other apps are intended to help as daily reminders.

Your phone doesn't have to be your enemy if you turn it into a weapon.

Make the choice to have your phone be a helpful tool rather than a harmful tool.

3. FIGHT IN THE DANGER ZONE

Tom Cruise made the Danger Zone seem exciting and fun as a fighter pilot in *Top Gun*. But the Danger Zone to which I am referring leads to failure and regret.

The Danger Zone is a relatively brief period of time when you find yourself more tempted than usual.

You're likely not tempted during all hours of the day. If you're like most guys, there comes a few moments throughout the day where seemingly out of nowhere, you're tempted more than usual. When you find yourself face-to-face with such a temptation, you're in the Danger Zone.

While the Danger Zone can easily lead toward a failure, the encouraging truth is that if you can occupy your mind for 30-45 minutes with something else when you find yourself in the Danger Zone, you'll likely get yourself out of it.

Research[12] shows that the desire for self-harm as a result of anxiety or suicidal thoughts often dissipates after 30-45 minutes. The same is true for lustful temptations.

In the moment of temptation, if you can preoccupy your mind for about a half hour, you have a much better chance of winning the battle for the day.

Each daily battle plan in this guide consists of a suggested Action Step you can use to help you push through the Danger Zone based on that day's challenge.

Implement an Action Step as soon as possible at the onset of a temptation. You might find that you enjoy some Action Steps, whereas others you may not. Go with your preference or simply what works. Use the same Action Steps over and over if you want.

Each day provides a new Action Step to keep things fresh, but don't feel as though you're limited to just that day's Action Step.

Use whatever step works for you to get yourself through the Danger Zone. Just make sure whatever action you take is safe and doesn't lead you toward some other type of temptation.

4. BUILD YOUR DEFENSE AND OFFENSE

Each day you are provided an opportunity to write down notes about how the enemy is coming at you. Similar to how football teams will watch film of their competition to learn their plays, keeping track of your enemy's tactics will help you know what's coming and how to fight against it.

While a solid defense is important, a solid offense can be even more important because getting yourself out of a tempting situation is much more difficult than avoiding the tempting situation altogether.

This guide will help you develop a solid defense and offense.

5. GENERATE MOMENTUM

By winning today's battle, you create momentum that will help you win tomorrow's battle. When you accumulate multiple days in a row, the momentum alone provides incentive to win the day.

The next section of this book is labeled "Streaks". Don't get too excited—this doesn't give you permission to tear off your clothes and run through the streets naked.

Streaks are intended to be a visual way of seeing multiple successful days in a row. There are several rows of streaks so if you give into temptation anytime while going through this book, you can continue reading where you left off the next day without starting the entire book over and simply create a new streak to generate new momentum.

Streaks will allow you to still capitalize on the power of momentum and positive habits while avoiding the need to re-read days you have already completed.

Regardless of the day of the month when you begin a new streak, strive to get all 31 days in a row in a single streak. That is the 31 Day Challenge—that you would refrain from PMO for 31 days in a row. Streaks will help you make that goal a reality.

I have also included several milestones along the way to help you celebrate longer streaks in your journey. The gray circles in your Streak tracker indicate each milestone.

If you find that streaks are helpful, you might consider downloading the free app HabitBull[13] onto your smart phone.

HabitBull allows you to create streak goals for whatever habits you want to make or break, and keeps your streak history on your mobile device well past the 31 days provided in this book. To download the free app, visit www.habitbull.com.

By incorporating these five tactics, you will be well on your way to winning your first battle with your personal battle plan.

Each day you'll be challenged with more ways to build your daily battle plan by customizing it more. By adding new ideas as you go, you will be creating a finely-tuned battle plan that will help you beat this enemy once and for all.

Let's do this.

GO STREAKING

Instructions: Fill in each successful day you win in a row to create a streak. Grey circles are milestones. If you have a setback, begin a new streak wherever you left off rather than starting over. You complete the #31daychallenge when you win 31 days in a row on a single streak.

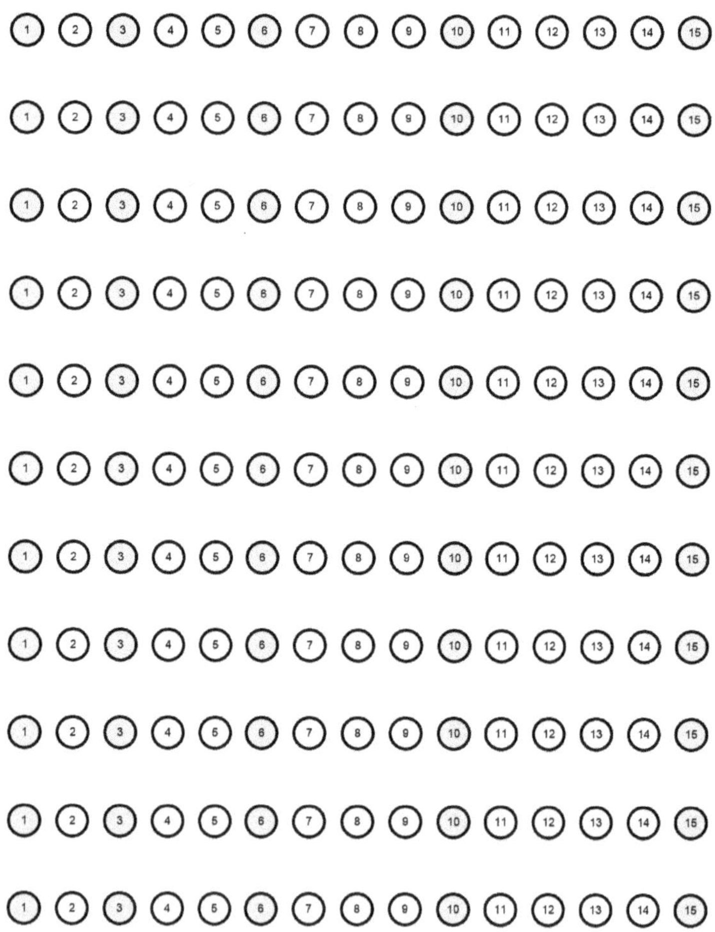

(Pro Tip: Accomplish the same streak goals on your smart phone by downloading the free HabitBull[13] app at www.habitbull.com.)

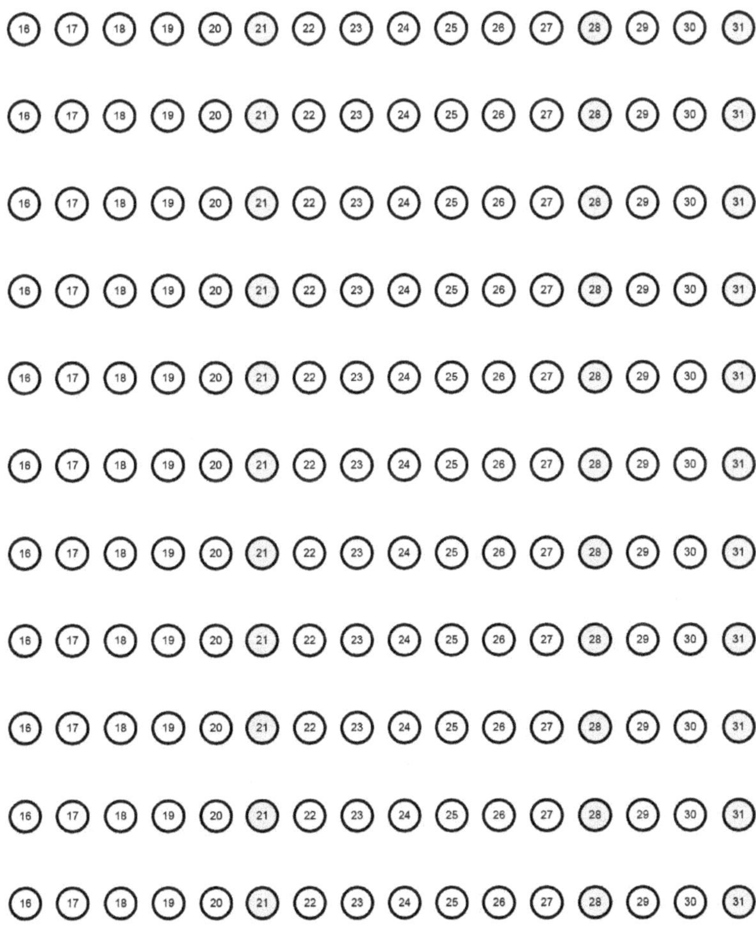

YOUR 31 DAY CHALLENGE BEGINS NOW

DAY 1

"Better to fight for something than live for nothing."
— George Patton

ENEMY TACTICS

Write down any enemy tactics or temptations you have faced recently. The more you study your enemy, the more you will recognize patterns in your enemy's warfare. The more you learn, the more prepared you will become and the more daily wins you will experience.

I'VE BEEN TEMPTED IN THE FOLLOWING WAYS IN THE LAST 24 HOURS:

____

____

____

THE FOLLOWING PEOPLE/PLACES/THINGS LEAD TO TEMPTING SITUATIONS:

____

____

____

ONE THING I CAN DO BASED ON WHAT I HAVE OBSERVED IS:

____

____

____

FACE YOUR ENEMY

This is a huge first step. Most people don't ever get this far because they simply don't want to make any effort. They want results without having to work for them.

Conquering your porn addiction will require strong action steps rather than passive good intentions. Props for taking action.

But here's the deal—you have an enemy who wants you to fail. The fact that you picked up this book and that you're reading this right now poses a threat to your enemy.

Any time you pose a threat to your enemy, it's not uncommon that you'll get attacked.

Be prepared for some sort of attack to come your way today. Maybe you get into a fight with a loved one and you feel more susceptible or vulnerable today. Maybe you find extra time on your hands and you get bored. Maybe some friends get mad at you for something.

Who knows what's coming your way, but you can be darn sure that your enemy does not want you to win this war.

Remember, the first step to winning the war is to win one battle at a time.

Before you can win today's battle, you've gotta know what you're up against. You're up against an enemy who hates you and wants you to fail at all costs.

Simply knowing there's someone out there who desperately wants you to mess this all up might actually help you knowing you can fight.

The gloves are off. No holding back. This means war.

TODAY'S TRUTH

"Your enemy the devil prowls around like a roaring lion looking for someone to devour." — **1 Peter 5:8**

TODAY'S ACTION STEP

Turn your phone into a weapon.

I'm not suggesting you throw it at your computer the next time something inappropriate pops up.

Instead, install an app or software to help you avoid temptation online. Some are free whereas others charge a fee.

Here are a few options:

- Covenant Eyes[15]
  Accountability software

- Chrome Safe Browser Plugin[16]
  Internet browser porn blocker

- X3 Watch[17]
  Accountability software

- K9 Web Protection[18]
  Internet browser porn blocker

- R|Tribe[19]
  Personal accountability app

CONGRATS!
YOU REACHED YOUR
1ST MILESTONE!
KEEP IT UP!

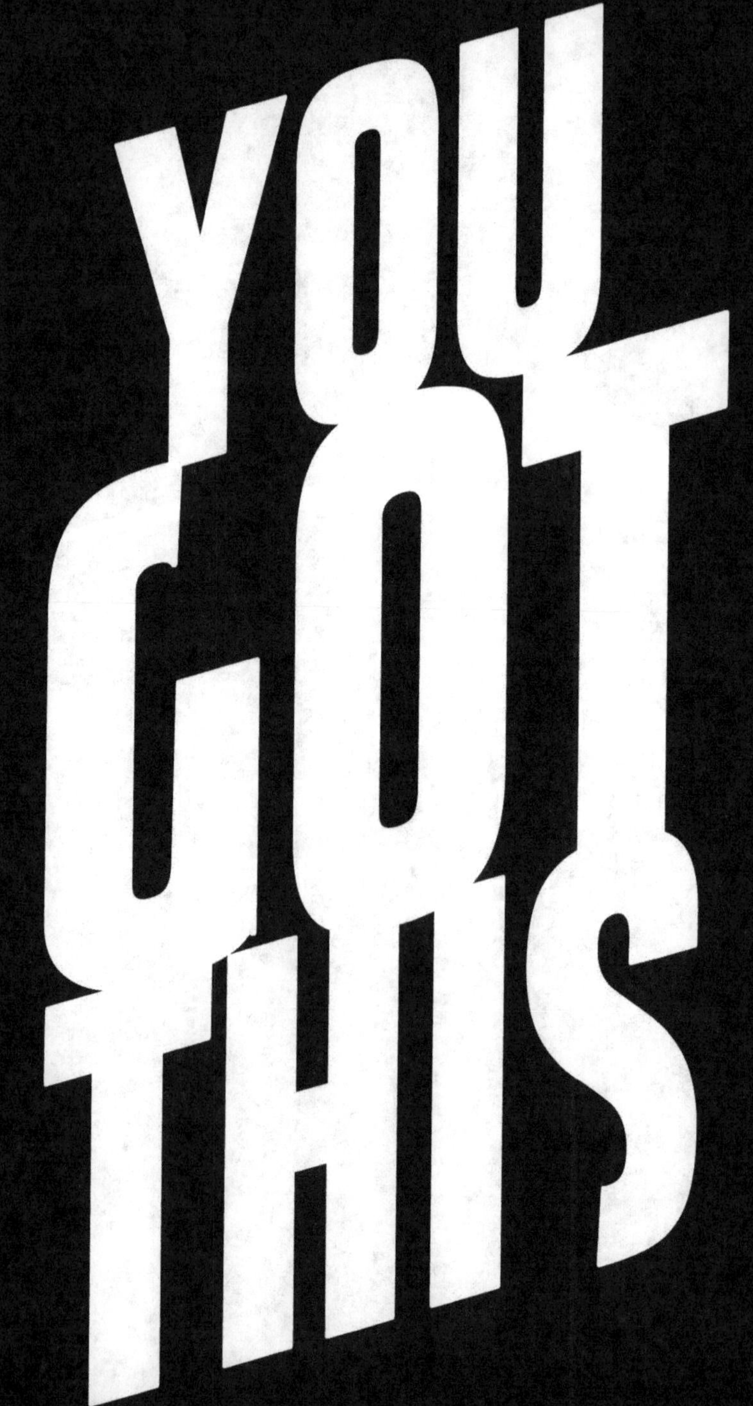

YOU
GOT
THIS

DAY 2

"Be strong, trust God's word, and trust the process."
— Germany Kent

ENEMY TACTICS

Write down any enemy tactics or temptations you have faced recently. The more you study your enemy, the more you will recognize patterns in your enemy's warfare. The more you learn, the more prepared you will become and the more daily wins you will experience.

I'VE BEEN TEMPTED IN THE FOLLOWING WAYS IN THE LAST 24 HOURS:

____

____

____

THE FOLLOWING PEOPLE/PLACES/THINGS LEAD TO TEMPTING SITUATIONS:

____

____

____

ONE THING I CAN DO BASED ON WHAT I HAVE OBSERVED IS:

____

____

____

SUBMIT TO GOD

Yesterday we learned about an enemy who wants us to fail. Unfortunately for our enemy, there is someone more powerful—God.

While you don't have to be a Christian to take the 31 Day Challenge, nothing else you've tried has helped you kick this habit so far, so why not give God a chance?

The secret of the Bible is that it was never meant to just be read. You've gotta actually do what it says[14] and take action.

If you do choose to trust in God and submit to the instructions He gives in the Bible, you could very well become free from the addiction you have fought for so long.

This entire guide incorporates and relies heavily on time-tried verses from the Bible. Whether you have faith in God or not, choose to trust the wisdom from the Bible for the next 31 days and see what happens.

TODAY'S TRUTH

"Submit yourselves, then, to God. Resist the devil, and he will flee from you." — **James 4:7**

TODAY'S ACTION STEP

Download the YouVersion Bible app.

The Bible says a lot about temptation and how to avoid it. Throughout this entire journey, you will be presented with Bible verses that can help you flee from your temptations.

The YouVersion app not only allows you to take the Bible with you wherever you go, but you can also highlight verses, bookmark verses, and make public or private notes about what stands out to you.

DAY 3

"An arrogant person considers himself perfect. This is the chief harm of arrogance. It interferes with a person's main task in life—becoming a better person."
— Leo Tolstoy

ENEMY TACTICS

Write down any enemy tactics or temptations you have faced recently. The more you study your enemy, the more you will recognize patterns in your enemy's warfare. The more you learn, the more prepared you will become and the more daily wins you will experience.

I'VE BEEN TEMPTED IN THE FOLLOWING WAYS IN THE LAST 24 HOURS:

____

____

____

THE FOLLOWING PEOPLE/PLACES/THINGS LEAD TO TEMPTING SITUATIONS:

____

____

____

ONE THING I CAN DO BASED ON WHAT I HAVE OBSERVED IS:

____

____

____

NOBODY'S PERFECT

We all fall short. Don't beat yourself up knowing that you're not perfect, because you simply can't hold yourself to that standard. In fact, you can't hold anyone to that standard.

There are plenty of other guys who not only struggle with the same things, but also want to rid their lives of unhealthy habits.

Knowing there are plenty of other guys dealing with the same thing, maybe it's time you brought some of them into this challenge.

TODAY'S TRUTH

"[F]or all have sinned and fall short of the glory of God..."
— Romans 3:23

TODAY'S ACTION STEP

Invite a few friends over to hang.

Board games, card games, it doesn't really matter.

On second thought, don't resort to drinking games. They'll mess up your decision making.

But think of a few friends who might enjoy hanging out and invite them over.

Today's Action Step is less about the fun you'll have from playing the games and more about teeing you up for tomorrow's Action Step.

CONGRATS!
YOU REACHED YOUR
2ND MILESTONE!
KEEP IT UP!

TRUST
THE
PROCESS

DAY 4

"God can't bless who you pretend to be."
— Steven Furtick

ENEMY TACTICS

Write down any enemy tactics or temptations you have faced recently. The more you study your enemy, the more you will recognize patterns in your enemy's warfare. The more you learn, the more prepared you will become and the more daily wins you will experience.

I'VE BEEN TEMPTED IN THE FOLLOWING WAYS IN THE LAST 24 HOURS:

____

____

____

THE FOLLOWING PEOPLE/PLACES/THINGS LEAD TO TEMPTING SITUATIONS:

____

____

____

ONE THING I CAN DO BASED ON WHAT I HAVE OBSERVED IS:

____

____

____

YOU AREN'T ALONE

Many people have a really difficult time with Day 4.

This is when you begin to miss what you gave up. However, the urge to relapse will dwindle if you stay strong.

Keep up the good work. If you have already failed by now, don't start over. Keep going. Each day that you have victory is one day closer to being completely free from this addiction.

Yesterday we were reminded that nobody is perfect and that everyone has some sort of baggage.

Knowing that you're not the only one facing this battle can be comforting. However, battles typically aren't won alone.

Battles require generals, pilots, soldiers, infantry, etc. The more guys you have fighting this battle alongside you, the more likely you will succeed.

It will take humility and vulnerability to be real with other guys about what's truly going on in your life.

CS Lewis said[20], *"Friendship is born at the moment when one man says to another "What! You too?"*

Could it be that there are other guys out there that are in dire need of someone to come alongside them and help them fight?

Not only do they need it—you need it.

Get the courage today to be real with someone else for a change.

TODAY'S TRUTH

"Therefore confess your sins to each other and pray for each other so that you may be healed. The prayer of a righteous person is powerful and effective."
— James 5:16

TODAY'S ACTION STEP

Make the big ask.

Call another guy, ask about the weather, ask how things are going, blaze through the small talk and cut to the chase. Let them know why you're *really* calling. Tell them all about this 31 Day Challenge, and ask them if they'll join you in the journey.

If they don't struggle with the same thing, then maybe you can gain some insight from them. If they do struggle with the same thing, then maybe they'll be down to jump into this challenge right along with you.

If you make the big ask, you'll have people in your corner who choose to run this race with you.

If they struggle with the same thing, but don't want to take on the challenge, keep asking other guys until you find one who's willing to fight alongside you.

DAY 5

*"If you tell a big enough lie and tell
it frequently enough, it will be believed."*
— **Adolf Hitler**

ENEMY TACTICS

Write down any enemy tactics or temptations you have faced recently. The more you study your enemy, the more you will recognize patterns in your enemy's warfare. The more you learn, the more prepared you will become and the more daily wins you will experience.

I'VE BEEN TEMPTED IN THE FOLLOWING WAYS IN THE LAST 24 HOURS:

____

____

____

THE FOLLOWING PEOPLE/PLACES/THINGS LEAD TO TEMPTING SITUATIONS:

____

____

____

ONE THING I CAN DO BASED ON WHAT I HAVE OBSERVED IS:

____

____

____

FATHER OF LIES

Behind every addiction is a lie. What is the lie you're believing? Maybe there is more than one.

The Bible describes our enemy as the "father of lies." How would you like that title?

One of the lies our enemy uses is that we just can't help ourselves. That the temptation is just too great, and that it's just a matter of time before we give in.

Don't buy it.

God promises there is ALWAYS a way out of every temptation. You might have to look for it, but it's there.

Search high, search low, but when you're tempted, find that way out!

Oftentimes the way out is simply occupying your mind with something else. Each day as you go through this book, be sure to implement the Action Step. Not only will it help you fight this war, but it's also designed to get you to focus on something else other than the temptation.

When you focus on something else, you trick your mind into spending energy on something else other than watching porn or engaging in other sexual sin.

TODAY'S TRUTH

"No temptation has overtaken you except what is common to mankind. And God is faithful; he will not let you be tempted beyond what you can bear. But when you are tempted, he will also provide a way out so that you can endure it." — **1 Corinthians 10:13**

TODAY'S ACTION STEP

Start a new project or hobby.

The idea is to find something you enjoy that can give you opportunities in the days to come to escape your inevitable temptations.

Ever been interested in woodcarving? Want to build something? Has your wife been asking for you to make something Pinteresty that can go on your living room wall?

There's gotta be something you've had a desire to do that you haven't yet tried. No, smoking weed for the first time because now it's legal in your state doesn't count.

Try to think of something you would enjoy working on that you likely won't finish in one sitting. This will give you the chance to whittle away on it, take a break, come back, and over time, finish your project.

DAY 6

"It is the part of a fool to give advice to others and not himself to be on his guard."
— **Phaedrus**

ENEMY TACTICS

Write down any enemy tactics or temptations you have faced recently. The more you study your enemy, the more you will recognize patterns in your enemy's warfare. The more you learn, the more prepared you will become and the more daily wins you will experience.

I'VE BEEN TEMPTED IN THE FOLLOWING WAYS IN THE LAST 24 HOURS:

____

____

____

THE FOLLOWING PEOPLE/PLACES/THINGS LEAD TO TEMPTING SITUATIONS:

____

____

____

ONE THING I CAN DO BASED ON WHAT I HAVE OBSERVED IS:

____

____

____

WORD OF CAUTION

If you and some friends installed accountability software that tracks websites you've each visited, good job! It's great you're being intentional about accountability!

While accountability is crucial, there is a possibility you might begin to receive emails containing clickable URLs of sites where your friends have been.

A word of caution: clicking some of the links may lead to innocent sites whereas clicking other links may lead to sexual content.

When reviewing browser history of your buddies, you must be on guard! Of course you can and should come alongside your friends and encourage them to avoid going to forbidden sites again, but you must be ready to close any browser windows that pop up content you shouldn't be viewing yourself.

Simply knowing what site they went to makes a search for porn much easier for you in a weak moment. Resist clicking on links that your friends also clicked, and don't get dragged into their same temptation.

TODAY'S TRUTH

"Brothers and sisters, if someone is caught in a sin, you who live by the Spirit should restore that person gently. But watch yourselves, or you also may be tempted."
— Galatians 6:1

TODAY'S ACTION STEP

Take a cold shower.

If the idea of a cold shower doesn't appeal to you at all, take a hot shower and switch it to cold for 30 seconds toward the end of your shower. Then switch it back and for from hot to cold several times. This little trick gets blood flowing and is actually good for you*.

Literally cooling down your body will not only allow your mind to focus on something else, but it also invigorates your body and gives you an energy boost[21].

In fact, it's actually a good idea to take a cold shower every day, not just when you're tempted.

Consult your doctor first if you have a history of heart problems.

CONGRATS!
YOU REACHED YOUR
3RD MILESTONE!
KEEP IT UP!

BE
ON
GUARD

DAY 7

"God is bigger than people think."
— **Jimmy Dean**

ENEMY TACTICS

Write down any enemy tactics or temptations you have faced recently. The more you study your enemy, the more you will recognize patterns in your enemy's warfare. The more you learn, the more prepared you will become and the more daily wins you will experience.

I'VE BEEN TEMPTED IN THE FOLLOWING WAYS IN THE LAST 24 HOURS:

THE FOLLOWING PEOPLE/PLACES/THINGS LEAD TO TEMPTING SITUATIONS:

ONE THING I CAN DO BASED ON WHAT I HAVE OBSERVED IS:

GREATER IS HE

Most guys want to be self-sufficient. They don't want help from others. It makes them feel incapable of achieving accomplishments on their own.

But if you believe that God created the heavens and the earth[22], then you must also believe that God's power is far greater than your own.

Shut out the pride that's keeping you from tapping into God's power.

Having God on your side will give you more strength than you'll ever have on your own.

TODAY'S TRUTH

"You, dear children, are from God and have overcome them, because the one who is in you is greater than the one who is in the world." — **1 John 4:4**

TODAY'S ACTION STEP

Lift weights.

Lifting weights actually creates tiny tears in your muscles, and as your body heals itself, your muscles get larger and your strength is increased.

If you don't have weights, you can use everyday items as alternatives, such as a gallon of milk, bags of oranges, bags of potatoes, bags of rice, etc.

Building physical strength can simultaneously help you build mental strength. As you see one area of your life improve, it will create a mental confidence that your entire life is improving.

DAY 8

"Go forth a conqueror and win great victories."
— Virgil

ENEMY TACTICS

Write down any enemy tactics or temptations you have faced recently. The more you study your enemy, the more you will recognize patterns in your enemy's warfare. The more you learn, the more prepared you will become and the more daily wins you will experience.

I'VE BEEN TEMPTED IN THE FOLLOWING WAYS IN THE LAST 24 HOURS:

____

____

____

THE FOLLOWING PEOPLE/PLACES/THINGS LEAD TO TEMPTING SITUATIONS:

____

____

____

ONE THING I CAN DO BASED ON WHAT I HAVE OBSERVED IS:

____

____

____

MORE THAN CONQUERORS

Think about how sweet victory will taste once you have conquered your enemy. Think about how it will feel to have this addiction a part of your past rather than part of your present. Think about how free you will feel when you've got a hold of this struggle.

Don't lie to yourself by saying this is an impossible challenge. It's not. It's been done—and it's been done by guys just like you.

You've got this.

This addiction *can* be conquered.

Don't give up.

And while you can definitely conquer your enemy and win this war, remind yourself that you are loved no matter what. You are more than a conqueror. You are loved.

TODAY'S TRUTH

"[I]n all these things we are more than conquerors through him who loved us." — **Romans 8:37**

TODAY'S WAY OUT

Move your furniture around.

This may sound ridiculous, but research shows[26] that people often fall into temptation and harmful habits based on predictability and routine.

If you switch things around your house, you are tricking your mind into subconsciously thinking that things are different than normal. You are breaking your routine.

Especially consider moving your typical spot that is associated with your previous PMO habits.

By simply moving your furniture around, you are decreasing your likelihood of slipping into old, comfortable habits.

DAY 9

*"No one knows the value of innocence
and integrity but he who has lost them."*
— William Godwin

ENEMY TACTICS

Write down any enemy tactics or temptations you have faced recently. The more you study your enemy, the more you will recognize patterns in your enemy's warfare. The more you learn, the more prepared you will become and the more daily wins you will experience.

I'VE BEEN TEMPTED IN THE FOLLOWING WAYS IN THE LAST 24 HOURS:

____

____

____

THE FOLLOWING PEOPLE/PLACES/THINGS LEAD TO TEMPTING SITUATIONS:

____

____

____

ONE THING I CAN DO BASED ON WHAT I HAVE OBSERVED IS:

____

____

____

FLEE FROM THIS

People don't respect someone who says one thing and then does another.

Strive to be a man of integrity and pursue attributes that others actually respect.

As you begin to run away from ungodly things, you naturally run toward godly things.

When your actions begin to align with your words, people will develop a greater respect for you.

TODAY'S TRUTH

"But you, man of God, flee from all this, and pursue righteousness, godliness, faith, love, endurance and gentleness." — **1 Timothy 6:11**

TODAY'S ACTION STEP

Go on a run.

A cardio workout does several positive things for you. A few of the obvious results are:

1.　You get your blood pumping
2.　You work off a bit of your gut
3.　You burn off all the donut calories you put down earlier this week

But in addition to the obvious, here are a few more positives of going on a run:

1.   You activate your adrenal glands. This is significant because you are releasing your energy in your workout rather than in unhealthy habits. At the end of your run, you will likely feel physically satisfied.

2.   You decrease anxiety. Studies show that anxiety and stress can be reduced by going on a run or doing some other type of cardio[27]. Oftentimes falling into sexual sin results from anxiety and stress. People will resort to bad sexual habits in the same way someone will go to drugs or alcohol in an unhealthy way to escape their reality. By reducing your anxiety and stress, you reduce your temptation.

3.   A run literally allows you to flee from your temptation. By creating positive repeating habits, such as fleeing the instant you face sexual temptation, the more it becomes second-hand nature to you. If you were to take this one Action Step and implement it each time you are tempted, there's a good chance you will successfully fight off every single temptation. It's that powerful.

Of course, if you don't like running or your knees are bad, you could replace it with any other cardio workout. Good alternatives could be mountain biking, road biking, swimming, elliptical machines, rollerblading, skateboarding, hiking, or anything else that elevates your heart rate.

When you do implement this Action Step, try to keep it up for at least 20-30 minutes to get the most out of it.

DAY 10

"The greatest gift is a portion of thyself."
— **Ralph Waldo Emerson**

ENEMY TACTICS

Write down any enemy tactics or temptations you have faced recently. The more you study your enemy, the more you will recognize patterns in your enemy's warfare. The more you learn, the more prepared you will become and the more daily wins you will experience.

I'VE BEEN TEMPTED IN THE FOLLOWING WAYS IN THE LAST 24 HOURS:

____

____

____

THE FOLLOWING PEOPLE/PLACES/THINGS LEAD TO TEMPTING SITUATIONS:

____

____

____

ONE THING I CAN DO BASED ON WHAT I HAVE OBSERVED IS:

____

____

____

FEEL ALIVE

Oftentimes Romans 6:23 is read in the context of the future, but it is also relevant in the present.

Sin doesn't just separate us from God; it separates us from others around us. The cost of sexual sin is a far greater price than most people are aware, but also a far greater cost than most people truly want to pay.

If you're able to banish the sin of lust from your daily life, you'll begin to feel alive again. You'll feel confidence come back again. You'll be living the type of life God wants you to live.

Sin makes you feel dead, but eradicating it will make you feel alive.

TODAY'S TRUTH

"For the wages of sin is death, but the gift of God is eternal life in Christ Jesus our Lord." — **Romans 6:23**

TODAY'S ACTION STEP

Cook a meal.

You've gotta eat, and most of us will do so at least three times a day. Rather than scavenging for whatever you can find, spend more time than you usually would to prepare your meal.

If you don't have the necessary ingredients, choose what you want to eat and then head to the store.

The entire process may take you an hour or more, but it will get you through the Danger Zone of your temptation, and at the end of your preparation, you also get a home-cooked meal!

If you don't know much about cooking, give baked ziti a shot if you like Italian. It happens to be my favorite meal and it seems impressive, but it is one of the easiest meals you can learn to make.

If you email me at matt@mattmizell.com, I'll send you my wife's recipe. You're welcome.

CONGRATS!
YOU REACHED YOUR
4TH MILESTONE!
KEEP IT UP!

WIN GREAT VICTORIES

DAY 11

*"Leadership is about taking
responsibility, not making excuses."*
— **Mitt Romney**

ENEMY TACTICS

Write down any enemy tactics or temptations you have faced recently. The more you study your enemy, the more you will recognize patterns in your enemy's warfare. The more you learn, the more prepared you will become and the more daily wins you will experience.

I'VE BEEN TEMPTED IN THE FOLLOWING WAYS IN THE LAST 24 HOURS:

____

____

____

THE FOLLOWING PEOPLE/PLACES/THINGS LEAD TO TEMPTING SITUATIONS:

____

____

____

ONE THING I CAN DO BASED ON WHAT I HAVE OBSERVED IS:

____

____

____

BY NO MEANS

It can be easy to justify the same sin when you've already done it once. "I've already slept with my girlfriend, so I might as well keep doing it." "I've already cheated on my spouse, so what's one more time?" "I already looked at porn this week, so I might as well do it again today."

Paul hits this justification on the head in his letter to the Romans. By continuing to sin just because you can ask for forgiveness later is an abuse of grace.

Grace is undeserved in the first place, so it's not that you earned it. But don't allow yourself to keep on sinning because God will forgive you anyways. Each time you sin, you are losing out in that moment what God could be doing in and through you instead.

Your time is too valuable to make excuses about throwing it away.

TODAY'S TRUTH

"What shall we say, then? Shall we go on sinning so that grace may increase? By no means! We are those who have died to sin; how can we live in it any longer?"
— **Romans 6:1-2**

TODAY'S ACTION STEP

Listen to a sermon.

There are countless sermons you can listen to. If you prefer to watch a video of one, do that instead.

So many people tend to justify their sinful actions because they think they've already messed up, so why not continue in it. The more you hear God's Word and those who teach it, the less likely you will be to make excuses for why you believe you're exempt from following it.

DAY 12

"The weak can never forgive. Forgiveness is an attribute of the strong."
— Mahatma Gandhi

ENEMY TACTICS

Write down any enemy tactics or temptations you have faced recently. The more you study your enemy, the more you will recognize patterns in your enemy's warfare. The more you learn, the more prepared you will become and the more daily wins you will experience.

I'VE BEEN TEMPTED IN THE FOLLOWING WAYS IN THE LAST 24 HOURS:

____

____

____

THE FOLLOWING PEOPLE/PLACES/THINGS LEAD TO TEMPTING SITUATIONS:

____

____

____

ONE THING I CAN DO BASED ON WHAT I HAVE OBSERVED IS:

____

____

____

UNCONDITIONAL FORGIVENESS

If you have messed up by now, be encouraged that God will forgive you for whatever you have done wrong. He is for you, not against you.

Remember it's not God that leads you into temptation. The enemy is looking for constant opportunities to lead you into evil. Thankfully God has the ability to lead you away from that evil.

Be thankful today that no matter what you do or don't do, God still offers His unconditional forgiveness.

TODAY'S TRUTH

"And forgive us our sins; for we also forgive every one that is indebted to us. And lead us not into temptation; but deliver us from evil." — **Luke 11:4 (KJV)**

TODAY'S ACTION STEP

Read a book.

Getting lost in a good book is a great way to get out of temptation. As your mind gets captivated by the plot and the characters, it's as if you mentally enter a different world and escape your own.

This is an especially helpful Action Step if you choose to read your book in a public place where you're less likely to put your book down and get yourself into trouble.

Grab a book you've been putting off reading, head to your local coffee shop, and spend about an hour of intentional and focused reading.

DAY 13

"My parents taught me to react quickly when temptation comes and to say 'No!' instantly and emphatically. I recommend that same counsel to you."
— Joseph Wirthlin

ENEMY TACTICS

Write down any enemy tactics or temptations you have faced recently. The more you study your enemy, the more you will recognize patterns in your enemy's warfare. The more you learn, the more prepared you will become and the more daily wins you will experience.

I'VE BEEN TEMPTED IN THE FOLLOWING WAYS IN THE LAST 24 HOURS:

____

____

____

THE FOLLOWING PEOPLE/PLACES/THINGS LEAD TO TEMPTING SITUATIONS:

____

____

____

ONE THING I CAN DO BASED ON WHAT I HAVE OBSERVED IS:

____

____

____

DO NOT ENTER

Jesus knew just how difficult it can be to get out of a tempting situation, so His challenge to His followers was to stay out of tempting situations altogether. It's much easier to refrain from entering a tempting situation than to get yourself out of a tempting situation.

While there is always a way out once you find yourself in a tempting situation, remind yourself today it's far better to stay away from the beginning.

What situations do you need to stay away from altogether? Maybe it's an exact location. Maybe it's a certain room. Maybe it's particular business. Maybe it's someone's house. Maybe it's listening to a certain type of music. Maybe it's watching a specific TV show.

Take a moment to think about what locations or triggers lead to your temptations, and pray that God will give you the strength and courage to avoid them.

TODAY'S TRUTH

"[He] said to them, 'Pray that you will not fall into temptation.'" — **Luke 22:40b**

TODAY'S ACTION STEP

Take a prayer walk.

Maybe you're into prayer, maybe not. Regardless, a prayer walk can help you focus your mind on things other than your temptation, or you can ask for God's supernatural strength to get you through your temptation.

Oftentimes the reason people don't pray is simply because they don't know how. It's not a mystery. Simply talk to God.

Some of my best prayer time is riding my motorcycle with my eyes wide open. There's no way I'm closing my eyes while riding my motorcycle, but because I'm not listening to a radio, I often use that time to talk with God.

Prayer doesn't have to be done exclusively when sitting in the pews of a church.

Take a walk, watch where you're going with your eyes wide open, and simply talk to God.

Tell Him what you're thankful for. Tell Him where you're struggling. Ask Him for strength. Pray for your family. Pray for your friends. Just be real by telling God your thoughts about what's going on in life.

A prayer walk will not just bring you closer in your relationship with God, but it will keep you from making poor decisions in the midst of a temptation.

DAY 14

"Never give in—never, never, never, never, in nothing great or small, large or petty. Never give in except to convictions of honor and good sense."
— Winston Churchill

ENEMY TACTICS

Write down any enemy tactics or temptations you have faced recently. The more you study your enemy, the more you will recognize patterns in your enemy's warfare. The more you learn, the more prepared you will become and the more daily wins you will experience.

I'VE BEEN TEMPTED IN THE FOLLOWING WAYS IN THE LAST 24 HOURS:

____

____

____

THE FOLLOWING PEOPLE/PLACES/THINGS LEAD TO TEMPTING SITUATIONS:

____

____

____

ONE THING I CAN DO BASED ON WHAT I HAVE OBSERVED IS:

____

____

____

KEEP WATCHING

The best defense is a good offense. Rather than relying on your ability to escape from a tempting situation, it is best to do your best to avoid getting into tempting situations in the first place.

To do this, you need to be honest with yourself about what situations tempt you most. Stressful times at work? Arguments at home? Being alone? Being alone with wifi? Being hungry? Being bored?

What are your "triggers"? Once you know your triggers, you will know what to avoid.

TODAY'S TRUTH

"Watch and pray so that you will not fall into temptation. The spirit is willing, but the flesh is weak."
— **Mark 14:38**

TODAY'S ACTION STEP

Watch a movie.

Similar to getting lost in the plot of a good book, watching a movie will allow you to mentally escape your tempting environment.

If possible, go to an actual movie theater so you're not inclined to pause the movie at home so you can jump back into your temptation.

By going to a public place to enjoy your movie, you are escaping your tempting environment.

Just make sure the movie you go to watch doesn't have any sexual scenes in it. If you aren't careful about the content that's in the movie, this Action Step could potentially lead you into an even tougher tempting situation by planting images in your mind that shouldn't be there.

DAY 15

"If you don't design your own life plan, chances are you'll fall into someone else's plan. And guess what they have planned for you? Not much."
— Jim Rohn

ENEMY TACTICS

Write down any enemy tactics or temptations you have faced recently. The more you study your enemy, the more you will recognize patterns in your enemy's warfare. The more you learn, the more prepared you will become and the more daily wins you will experience.

I'VE BEEN TEMPTED IN THE FOLLOWING WAYS IN THE LAST 24 HOURS:

____

____

____

THE FOLLOWING PEOPLE/PLACES/THINGS LEAD TO TEMPTING SITUATIONS:

____

____

____

ONE THING I CAN DO BASED ON WHAT I HAVE OBSERVED IS:

____

____

____

YOUR SECRET WEAPON

There's a story[23] in the Bible where two guys named Paul and Silas were stripped, beaten and imprisoned simply for following God.

While in prison, they began to sing worship songs. I'm not sure if that's the time or place I'd feel like singing, but these guys chose to worship God even in the midst of an incredibly difficult trial.

As it turned out, their songs of praise started a series of events that eventually led not only to being freed from prison, but it also led others to Jesus.

Worship is your secret weapon. It can break chains and lead to freedom. Not only does it focus you on an all-powerful God, but it also leads others to that same God.

However, be sure that it is God whom you are worshipping. It is important to understand that freedom from your addiction will likely not come as a result of a series of commitments, memorized scriptures, conversations with accountability partners, or any other form of self-help.

This book is not intended to be the actual tool to set you free, but simply a guide designed to lead you to the God and Savior who can.

TODAY'S TRUTH

"Jesus said to him, 'Away from me, Satan! For it is written: 'Worship the Lord your God, and serve him only.'''" — **Matthew 4:10**

TODAY'S ACTION STEP

Worship.

By actively thinking of things for which you're thankful, you are challenging your mind to think of other positive and healthy things in your life.

You could sing a song of praise to God just how Paul and Silas did when they held in prison. However, worship isn't limited to just singing songs.

Worship is anything you do to bring honor and glory to God. An act of worship could be an activity, the way you treat someone, creating something, giving something—there truly is no limit to how you can worship.

Regardless of the way you choose to worship, give the best absolute best you've got in whatever it is.

CONGRATS!
YOU REACHED YOUR
5TH MILESTONE!
KEEP IT UP!

NEVER
GIVE
IN

DAY 16

"The opposite of anger is not calmness, it's empathy."
— Mehmet Oz

ENEMY TACTICS

Write down any enemy tactics or temptations you have faced recently. The more you study your enemy, the more you will recognize patterns in your enemy's warfare. The more you learn, the more prepared you will become and the more daily wins you will experience.

I'VE BEEN TEMPTED IN THE FOLLOWING WAYS IN THE LAST 24 HOURS:

____

____

____

THE FOLLOWING PEOPLE/PLACES/THINGS LEAD TO TEMPTING SITUATIONS:

____

____

____

ONE THING I CAN DO BASED ON WHAT I HAVE OBSERVED IS:

____

____

____

DRAW NEAR

Not only do millions of others face the same temptations, but even Jesus Himself faced temptation.

Jesus was still God when He was tempted, so you might be inclined to think, "Well of course He didn't sin! He was God!"

While that is true, Jesus is at least familiar with the struggle. He knows what it feels like to be tempted. He doesn't just offer sympathy, but He offers empathy. He knows the strength and power of temptation. He also knows that it is possible to fight off each temptation.

It can be helpful to know you're not the only one who struggles with fighting battles each day. Hopefully you have been connecting with other guys and holding them accountable as they do the same for you.

Just because other guys face the same struggle does not, however, justify your actions. Don't buy into the lie that because you're not alone, that somehow it's okay. It's not.

Oh, and by the way, you're over halfway done with the 31 Day Challenge! Keep going!

TODAY'S TRUTH

"For we do not have a high priest who cannot sympathize with our weaknesses, but One who has been tempted in all things as we are, yet without sin. Therefore let us draw near with confidence to the throne of grace, so that we may receive mercy and find grace to help in time of need."
— Hebrews 4:15-16 (NASB)

TODAY'S ACTION STEP

Write a thank you card.

Yesterday's Action Step was to worship. Oftentimes when we worship, we think of things for which we're thankful.

Today, take that one step further by pinpointing someone who has blessed you in some way. Maybe they gave you a gift, but maybe you're just thankful for time they have given you or you're thankful for their friendship.

Take a few moments today to write a thank you card to someone who has done something kind to you. Not only are you paying it forward with their kindness, but you're refocusing your mind to get out your temptation.

DAY 17

"Set a goal and don't quit until you attain it."
— Bear Brandt

ENEMY TACTICS

Write down any enemy tactics or temptations you have faced recently. The more you study your enemy, the more you will recognize patterns in your enemy's warfare. The more you learn, the more prepared you will become and the more daily wins you will experience.

I'VE BEEN TEMPTED IN THE FOLLOWING WAYS IN THE LAST 24 HOURS:

____

____

____

THE FOLLOWING PEOPLE/PLACES/THINGS LEAD TO TEMPTING SITUATIONS:

____

____

____

ONE THING I CAN DO BASED ON WHAT I HAVE OBSERVED IS:

____

____

____

YOUR WAY OUT

You don't have to give in to your temptation.

Since Jesus was tempted way before you were ever tempted, He can help you find your way out. Continue each day to read the truth from the Bible so you can apply godly wisdom to your life.

Remember, a temptation itself isn't a sin. What you do with a temptation determines whether you sin or not.

TODAY'S TRUTH

"Because He Himself suffered when He was tempted, He is able to help those who are being tempted."
— **Hebrews 2:18**

TODAY'S ACTION STEP

Text an accountability partner.

Remember the guys you talked to back on Day 4? Reach out to them. Send them a text.

The single biggest reason accountability doesn't work for most men is they choose an accountability partner, but then never actually reach out to them to hold them accountable.

Accountability simply doesn't work if neither person is willing to be the one to initiate the conversation.

If you haven't heard from them in a while, there's a good chance they need the accountability even more than you.

Don't fail them by being silent or passive. Initiate the conversation with at least one of your friends right now.

DAY 18

*"Accept the challenges so you can
feel the exhilaration of victory."*
— George Patton

ENEMY TACTICS

Write down any enemy tactics or temptations you have faced recently. The more you study your enemy, the more you will recognize patterns in your enemy's warfare. The more you learn, the more prepared you will become and the more daily wins you will experience.

I'VE BEEN TEMPTED IN THE FOLLOWING WAYS IN THE LAST 24 HOURS:

____

____

____

THE FOLLOWING PEOPLE/PLACES/THINGS LEAD TO TEMPTING SITUATIONS:

____

____

____

ONE THING I CAN DO BASED ON WHAT I HAVE OBSERVED IS:

____

____

____

OH SO SWEET

This fight will all be worth it in the end. Once you have conquered the enemy in this war and have victory, you will experience life in a completely new way.

This isn't to say the battle won't continue to be hard. It will be. But keep fighting. Keep pushing. Keep persevering. No pain, no gain.

The taste of victory is oh so sweet.

TODAY'S TRUTH

"Blessed is the one who perseveres under trial because, having stood the test, that person will receive the crown of life that the Lord has promised to those who love him."
— James 1:12

TODAY'S ACTION STEP

Go to the gym.

If you don't have a gym, do as many push-ups on your floor as you can before your arms give out.

Right when you feel like you have nothing else to give, give a little bit more. It is in this painful phase of a workout that most of the benefit is done to your body. If you feel like you can't go any further, go a little bit more.

Not only are you benefitting your body, but you are mentally conditioning yourself to know that when you feel like you have nothing left, you can still push through.

This is an important truth to remember about temptation. When you feel like there's nothing else you can do, there is. Keep pushing. Keep fighting. By making that final push to get out of a temptation or through it, you may very well find your freedom on the other side.

In addition to the psychological benefits of a workout, exercise will boost endorphins that will also make you feel good.

Feeling good about yourself is one of the best ways to fight your daily battle.

DAY 19

"Efforts and courage are not enough without purpose and direction."
— **John F. Kennedy**

ENEMY TACTICS

Write down any enemy tactics or temptations you have faced recently. The more you study your enemy, the more you will recognize patterns in your enemy's warfare. The more you learn, the more prepared you will become and the more daily wins you will experience.

I'VE BEEN TEMPTED IN THE FOLLOWING WAYS IN THE LAST 24 HOURS:

____

____

____

THE FOLLOWING PEOPLE/PLACES/THINGS LEAD TO TEMPTING SITUATIONS:

____

____

____

ONE THING I CAN DO BASED ON WHAT I HAVE OBSERVED IS:

____

____

____

MASTER OVER YOU

You're a tool.

Not in the negative sense of the word. Your body is a tool. Not only does each body part have specific uses, but you yourself have a specific purpose.

God has a plan for you. But God is good and holy, which means that He obviously isn't down with you using the body He created and gifted to you for unholy actions.

Each day as you become more submissive to God and reliant upon His power and His truths in your life, the less control and grip your lust will have over your life.

Keep fighting.

TODAY'S TRUTH

"Therefore do not let sin reign in your mortal body so that you obey its lusts, and do not go on presenting the members of your body to sin as instruments of unrighteousness; but present yourselves to God as those alive from the dead, and your members as instruments of righteousness to God. For sin shall not be master over you, for you are not under law but under grace."
— Romans 6:12-14 (NASB)

TODAY'S ACTION STEP

Check your tire pressure.

Today's Action Step challenges you to use a tool to do something relatively simple that could save you money or even your life.

We often don't think about tire pressure all that often, but if your tires aren't inflated properly you decrease your gas mileage.

Poorly inflated tires can also lead to blowouts, and in some tragic cases, blowouts have led to deaths resulting from rollovers or accidents while drivers are changing tires on the side of the road.

These are rare and extreme situations, but the reality is that a simple tool like a tire gauge can help you save money and prevent heartache.

Using this tool today in your Action Step is simply a reminder that your body is also a tool, and when used properly, it can also save you time and money when using your body in the way it was designed to be used.

DAY 20

*"Honor commitments, and they
will double back to honor you."*
— **Bill Rancic**

ENEMY TACTICS

Write down any enemy tactics or temptations you have faced recently. The more you study your enemy, the more you will recognize patterns in your enemy's warfare. The more you learn, the more prepared you will become and the more daily wins you will experience.

I'VE BEEN TEMPTED IN THE FOLLOWING WAYS IN THE LAST 24 HOURS:

____

____

____

THE FOLLOWING PEOPLE/PLACES/THINGS LEAD TO TEMPTING SITUATIONS:

____

____

____

ONE THING I CAN DO BASED ON WHAT I HAVE OBSERVED IS:

____

____

____

MAKE THE PROMISE

In our culture today, making a promise doesn't mean much. People break their word just as quickly as they make it.

Let people do whatever they want, but for you, you've got to convince yourself that your word matters. It does matter.

Jesus said[24], "Let your word 'yes' be 'yes,' and your 'no' be 'no.'"

Solomon said[25], "It is better not to make a vow than to make one and not fulfill it."

Choose right now that your word will mean something. Don't make promises you don't intend to keep.

That being said, you need to make a promise right now. Promise yourself that you will STOP looking at women lustfully.

Don't make this promise if you don't intend to follow through with it. If you are ready to put this addiction behind you, you've got to make a commitment that you have every intention of honoring.

Go ahead… make the promise.

TODAY'S TRUTH

"I made a covenant with my eyes not to look lustfully at a young woman." — **Job 31:1**

TODAY'S ACTION STEP

Call a friend.

This sounds like a game show option to phone a friend.

However, today's Action Step is different from Day 17 because the friend you call today doesn't have to be someone who has agreed to hold you accountable. You aren't calling for the sake of assistance in your struggle today; you are calling your friend simply to catch up.

Oftentimes I don't do a great job keeping in touch with people whom I consider to be my friends. This is especially true of friends I know who now live in other states.

Follow through with your commitment to be a friend by being intentional and calling someone with whom you haven't spoken in a while.

DAY 21

*"The great enemy of the truth is very
often not the lie, deliberate, contrived and dishonest,
but the myth, persistent, persuasive and unrealistic."*
— John F. Kennedy

ENEMY TACTICS

Write down any enemy tactics or temptations you have faced recently. The more you study your enemy, the more you will recognize patterns in your enemy's warfare. The more you learn, the more prepared you will become and the more daily wins you will experience.

I'VE BEEN TEMPTED IN THE FOLLOWING WAYS IN THE LAST 24 HOURS:

____

____

____

THE FOLLOWING PEOPLE/PLACES/THINGS LEAD TO TEMPTING SITUATIONS:

____

____

____

ONE THING I CAN DO BASED ON WHAT I HAVE OBSERVED IS:

____

____

____

SMOOTH TALK

Lust is a slippery slope.

Without even realizing it, allowing yourself to simply glance or gaze at a woman may lead to incredible damage.

We already know it is much more difficult to escape from a tempting situation than to avoid getting into one altogether. That's why it is super important to be able to recognize what traps look like.

The more you pay attention to what gets you into trouble, the more you'll be able to avoid traps that are deceitfully innocent on the outside.

TODAY'S TRUTH

"With persuasive words she led him astray; she seduced him with her smooth talk. All at once he followed her like an ox going to the slaughter, like a deer stepping into a noose till an arrow pierces his liver, like a bird darting into a snare, little knowing it will cost him his life."
— **Proverbs 7:21-23**

TODAY'S ACTION STEP

Create a playlist.

Go to Spotify or Amazon and add a bunch of songs from your favorite artists. Maybe even make a playlist that relates to conquering your struggle, so anytime you find yourself being tempted, you can plug in your headphones and go do another Action Step in addition to listening to some of your favorite music.

By filling your mind with music, you can escape today's temptations as you focus on something else.

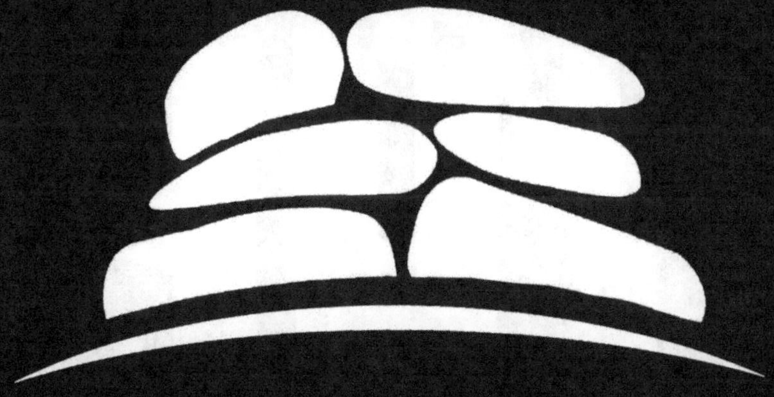

CONGRATS!
YOU REACHED YOUR
6TH MILESTONE!
KEEP IT UP!

STAND THE TEST

DAY 22

"What we seek we shall find.
What we flee from flees from us."
— Ralph Waldo Emerson

ENEMY TACTICS

Write down any enemy tactics or temptations you have faced recently. The more you study your enemy, the more you will recognize patterns in your enemy's warfare. The more you learn, the more prepared you will become and the more daily wins you will experience.

I'VE BEEN TEMPTED IN THE FOLLOWING WAYS IN THE LAST 24 HOURS:

____

____

____

THE FOLLOWING PEOPLE/PLACES/THINGS LEAD TO TEMPTING SITUATIONS:

____

____

____

ONE THING I CAN DO BASED ON WHAT I HAVE OBSERVED IS:

____

____

____

THIS GREAT EVIL

If you aren't familiar with the story of Joseph, it's worth going back and reading the entire story. It's one of the most inspirational stories of the entire Bible when it comes to fleeing temptation.

In today's verses, we look at just how tempting it can be if another woman comes onto you.

A woman who says "Lie with me" isn't asking you to be deceitful; she's asking you to sleep with her. A woman who says "Take me" isn't asking you to drop her off somewhere; she's asking you to have sex with her.

If you are married, you could have no intention of getting into an affair, but if another woman comes onto you, writes you a love letter or expresses her love for you in some other way, you skyrocket to a 90% chance of infidelity[28].

The solution? Transparency.

If someone other than your spouse ever reveals her love to you, tell your spouse immediately! In addition, you must sever any friendship you have with that person. Even if they are family friends, you cannot stay in the presence of temptation. It is too risky, and you have too much at stake.

Take a lesson from Joseph and run.

TODAY'S TRUTH

"It came about after these events that his master's wife looked with desire at Joseph, and she said, 'Lie with me.' But he refused and said to his master's wife, 'Behold, with me here, my master does not concern himself with anything in the house, and he has put all that he owns in my charge. There is no one greater in this house than I, and he has withheld nothing from me except you, because you are his wife. How then could I do this great evil and sin against God?'" — **Genesis 39:7-10 (NASB)**

TODAY'S ACTION STEP

Clean out your closet.

Getting rid of stuff you don't wear is a good exercise to go through each year. If you haven't worn something in a year, donate it.

This Action Step is also a good mental metaphor that you shouldn't have hidden sins or hold onto things that aren't good for you.

Out with the old destructive habits, in with the new healthy habits.

DAY 23

*"If you want to do something, then you should go all
out."*
— **Anushka Sharma**

ENEMY TACTICS

Write down any enemy tactics or temptations you have faced recently. The more you study your enemy, the more you will recognize patterns in your enemy's warfare. The more you learn, the more prepared you will become and the more daily wins you will experience.

I'VE BEEN TEMPTED IN THE FOLLOWING WAYS IN THE LAST 24 HOURS:

____

____

____

THE FOLLOWING PEOPLE/PLACES/THINGS LEAD TO TEMPTING SITUATIONS:

____

____

____

ONE THING I CAN DO BASED ON WHAT I HAVE OBSERVED IS:

____

____

____

EXTREME MEASURES

As a teenager struggling with an addiction to porn, I would read today's verse and actually consider if Jesus was telling me to literally gouge out my eye or cut off my hand. Crazy, right?

In hindsight I am grateful I didn't go to such extremes. However, I do believe Jesus wants us to indeed take extreme measures. While castrating yourself may be the ultimate extreme measure, I don't think taking such an action is the best option.

What kind of extreme measure should you take?

Maybe you need to get rid of your laptop. Maybe you need to leave it in your locker or at work so you don't have access to it. Maybe you need to get a dumb phone that doesn't have access to the internet or images. Maybe you need to kill the wifi in your house after 9pm.

There are several extreme measures you can take without damaging the gifts and plans God has for you down the road.

Desperate times call for desperate measures.

TODAY'S TRUTH

"If your hand or your foot causes you to stumble, cut it off and throw it from you; it is better for you to enter life crippled or lame, than to have two hands or two feet and be cast into the eternal fire. If your eye causes you to stumble, pluck it out and throw it from you It is better for you to enter life with one eye, than to have two eyes and be cast into the fiery hell." **— Matthew 18:8-9 (NASB)**

TODAY'S ACTION STEP

Do 30 burpees.

Don't know what a "burpee" is? Google it.

It's a type of workout that seems simple enough, but I can pretty much guarantee it will make you sore.

A buddy of mine who was a workout trainer agreed to train me for free after I bumped into him at a gym several years ago. He made me do several different types of workouts, and the circuit ended with several sets of burpees.

The next day I could barely walk.

For fitness gurus, burpees may be just a normal workout. But for others, a round of burpees may be an extreme workout given how sore you will be the next day.

If you are sore, allow that soreness to be a reminder that you successfully fought off your temptation.

DAY 24

"Whenever the strength of God is not recognized as the source of our strength, we are breaking the First Commandment: 'Do not have any gods before me.'"
— John Piper

ENEMY TACTICS

Write down any enemy tactics or temptations you have faced recently. The more you study your enemy, the more you will recognize patterns in your enemy's warfare. The more you learn, the more prepared you will become and the more daily wins you will experience.

I'VE BEEN TEMPTED IN THE FOLLOWING WAYS IN THE LAST 24 HOURS:

____

____

____

THE FOLLOWING PEOPLE/PLACES/THINGS LEAD TO TEMPTING SITUATIONS:

____

____

____

ONE THING I CAN DO BASED ON WHAT I HAVE OBSERVED IS:

____

____

____

DISPLAY STRENGTH

You might have friends who are also going through this battle against porn.

However, other guys may not look at it for what it is. They may try to convince you that porn is healthy. That it allows for a release. That it's not hurting anyone else.

Don't buy into the lies, even if they sound convincing. The enemy wants you to make light of it, but it is destructive and damaging. Anyone who tells you otherwise is naïve to the truth, simply deceived or just wants to justify continuing in their own sin.

TODAY'S TRUTH

"By smooth words he will turn to godlessness those who act wickedly toward the covenant, but the people who know their God will display strength and take action."
— Daniel 11:32 (NASB)

TODAY'S ACTION STEP

Fix something.

The key phrase from today's verse: "take action".

A girl I knew in high school had been given a used Camaro for her 16th birthday.

Her car was the envy of many guys in the school… that is, until we saw her on the side of the highway one day with smoke billowing from her raised hood.

It turns out that her oil light had come on months earlier, but that she simply ignored it.

By ignoring what at the time was a small problem, it turned into a huge problem when her engine locked up and caught on fire.

The damage to her engine would cost more than the cost of her Camaro, and because she naïvely neglected to fix a small problem, her car was totaled because it turned into a big problem.

There's probably a list of things around the house that you know you need to fix, but you simply haven't taken action.

I know, I know… you're busy. You've got plenty of other things going on.

But with today's Action Step, taking action by fixing something around the house will be a mental reminder that you must take action in your fight against porn early before your small issue becomes a big issue.

By choosing to *not* take action, little things that could have been fixed turn into bigger problems.

DAY 25

*"A leader takes people where they want
to go. A great leader takes people where they
don't necessarily want to go, but ought to be."*
— Rosalynn Carter

ENEMY TACTICS

Write down any enemy tactics or temptations you have faced recently. The more you study your enemy, the more you will recognize patterns in your enemy's warfare. The more you learn, the more prepared you will become and the more daily wins you will experience.

I'VE BEEN TEMPTED IN THE FOLLOWING WAYS IN THE LAST 24 HOURS:

____

____

____

THE FOLLOWING PEOPLE/PLACES/THINGS LEAD TO TEMPTING SITUATIONS:

____

____

____

ONE THING I CAN DO BASED ON WHAT I HAVE OBSERVED IS:

____

____

____

MAKE UP YOUR MIND

Your standard should be what God says rather than what society says. What comes out of Hollywood indicates that sexual promiscuity is the cultural norm. Unfortunately, it *is* the cultural norm.

Did you know that the porn industry makes more money than all American professional sports industries[29] COMBINED?! Porn generates[30] nearly $100 billion in annual sales worldwide!

That's an insane amount of profit being made each year based on vulgarity. Don't get caught in the web of what others are doing. Make up your mind that you won't just follow the crowd's actions, but that you'll blaze a new trail if necessary.

The interesting thing is… should you choose to blaze a new trail, you'll soon discover that others are willing to follow. They're waiting to follow. People want a leader. While some people lead down the path toward destruction, if you head down a path of godliness, others around you will follow.

Be a leader worth following.

TODAY'S TRUTH

"But Daniel resolved not to defile himself with the royal food and wine, and he asked the chief official for permission not to defile himself this way."
— **Daniel 1:8**

TODAY'S ACTION STEP

Sharpen your leadership skills.

Download a free leadership book called *The Secret to Success* at www.mattmizell.com/success.

This quick read will help you learn how to use the passions, skills and experience God has given you to more effectively lead others around you.

DAY 26

*"The only way you can serve God
is by serving other people."*
— **Rick Warren**

ENEMY TACTICS

Write down any enemy tactics or temptations you have faced recently. The more you study your enemy, the more you will recognize patterns in your enemy's warfare. The more you learn, the more prepared you will become and the more daily wins you will experience.

I'VE BEEN TEMPTED IN THE FOLLOWING WAYS IN THE LAST 24 HOURS:

____

____

____

THE FOLLOWING PEOPLE/PLACES/THINGS LEAD TO TEMPTING SITUATIONS:

____

____

____

ONE THING I CAN DO BASED ON WHAT I HAVE OBSERVED IS:

____

____

____

INNOCENT BLOOD

Many people get into sin because they have nothing else going on. They get bored, so they try to fill their boredom with things that might bring a thrill.

Truth be told, sin *is* fun. For a time. That fun is fleeting, and then you're left with a world of pain and hurt and shame.

Rather than occupy your free time by doing stupid stuff, try occupying your free time with things that actually benefit others. Look for ways to serve. Serve your family. Serve your friends. Serve your church. Serve your community.

By doing something beneficial with your free time, you'll not only be a blessing to others, but you'll keep yourself free from the misery of regret that comes after a fall.

TODAY'S TRUTH

"My son, if sinful men entice you, do not give in to them. If they say, "Come along with us; let's lie in wait for innocent blood, let's ambush some harmless soul'; my son, do not go along with them, do not set foot on their paths; for their feet rush into evil, they are swift to shed blood."
— Proverbs 1:10-11, 15-16

TODAY'S ACTION STEP

Donate blood.

Today's verse mentions those who are quick to take the blood of others, but it's another thing to willingly give up your blood in order to help others.

Find a local blood bank and head in to offer up your blood as a way to serve those whom you will never even meet. Doing so will be using your body as a way to bless others.

DAY 27

"Don't let yourself make excuses for not doing the things you want to do."
— **Sam Altman**

ENEMY TACTICS

Write down any enemy tactics or temptations you have faced recently. The more you study your enemy, the more you will recognize patterns in your enemy's warfare. The more you learn, the more prepared you will become and the more daily wins you will experience.

I'VE BEEN TEMPTED IN THE FOLLOWING WAYS IN THE LAST 24 HOURS:

____

____

____

THE FOLLOWING PEOPLE/PLACES/THINGS LEAD TO TEMPTING SITUATIONS:

____

____

____

ONE THING I CAN DO BASED ON WHAT I HAVE OBSERVED IS:

____

____

____

CONSISTENTLY HONORABLE

I've heard it said that if you're not in a storm, you either just came out of one or you're heading into one.

Bad days are coming, and bad days can be crippling when it comes to the war against porn. Make the decision right now that no matter what type of day you face, your fight against porn won't waiver.

If you lose a separate battle in another area of your life, it doesn't mean you should throw in the towel and lose *all* battles in your life.

Job was a guy in the Bible who faced some horrific days. Yet despite the worst days he could possibly imagine, he chose not to sin on those days.

When you have a tough day, tell someone about it. Vent to a friend. Go on a run. But do not use the horrible day as an excuse to jump into sin.

Bad days will come and go, but what we're fighting for is a consistently honorable lifestyle no matter what the day brings.

TODAY'S TRUTH

"In all of this, Job did not sin by blaming God."
— Job 1:22 (NLT)

TODAY'S ACTION STEP

Floss.

Consistency is crucial in your fight against PMO. Speak to any dentist, and they'll tell you consistency in flossing is just as crucial.

For years, I have viewed flossing as boring and inconvenient, so I just didn't do it.

Just recently I have picked it up and tried to be consistent with it.

By creating other positive consistent habits, you will also gain traction with positive consistency against your unhealthy habits as well.

DAY 28

"There's no destination. The journey is all that there is, and it can be very, very joyful."
— **Srikumar Rao**

ENEMY TACTICS

Write down any enemy tactics or temptations you have faced recently. The more you study your enemy, the more you will recognize patterns in your enemy's warfare. The more you learn, the more prepared you will become and the more daily wins you will experience.

I'VE BEEN TEMPTED IN THE FOLLOWING WAYS IN THE LAST 24 HOURS:

____

____

____

THE FOLLOWING PEOPLE/PLACES/THINGS LEAD TO TEMPTING SITUATIONS:

____

____

____

ONE THING I CAN DO BASED ON WHAT I HAVE OBSERVED IS:

____

____

____

CONSIDER IT PURE JOY

Facing trials can be difficult, but those trials help you build character and endurance. Every trial is a learning opportunity.

Look at this war the same way. What can you learn about yourself? What can you learn about others? About those who are closest to you? About this particular temptation in general?

The more you learn about your specific trials, two things happen:

1. You learn more about how to avoid the same situations in the future, and

2. You are capable of providing hope to others who are just beginning to face the same trial.

God is in the business of making dirty things beautiful. Allow Him to use your story to strengthen your future and the future of others.

TODAY'S TRUTH

"Consider it pure joy, my brothers and sisters, whenever you face trials of many kinds, because you know that the testing of your faith produces perseverance."
— James 1:2-3

TODAY'S ACTION STEP

Wash your car.

Today's Action Step is a metaphorical reminder that God can make dirty things beautiful again.

After you wash your car, the next time you get in it, you will have a visual example of seeing how what was once dirty can be cleaned.

Don't have a car? Wash your parent's car. Wash your friend's car. Be a blessing and bring joy to someone else.

Knowing that God provides grace and redemption despite the failures within our trials is something that also brings joy.

CONGRATS!
YOU REACHED YOUR
7TH MILESTONE!
KEEP IT UP!

GO
ALL
OUT

DAY 29

*"Success does not consist in never making mistakes,
but in never making the same one a second time."*
— **George Bernard Shaw**

ENEMY TACTICS

Write down any enemy tactics or temptations you have faced recently. The more you study your enemy, the more you will recognize patterns in your enemy's warfare. The more you learn, the more prepared you will become and the more daily wins you will experience.

I'VE BEEN TEMPTED IN THE FOLLOWING WAYS IN THE LAST 24 HOURS:

____

____

____

THE FOLLOWING PEOPLE/PLACES/THINGS LEAD TO TEMPTING SITUATIONS:

____

____

____

ONE THING I CAN DO BASED ON WHAT I HAVE OBSERVED IS:

____

____

____

BE ON GUARD

Now that you have come this far, the enemy is likely taking notice and may come at you with a greater intensity. Do your best to stay strong. Be on guard.

Paul warned[31] us that when we think we're strong, we are actually vulnerable to attacks.

The benefit you have is that you know the tactics of the enemy. You have studied his moves for nearly a month now, and you probably have a pretty good idea of where and how he will attack you with temptation.

A simple mistake can lead to a significant relapse. Be on guard so you don't make errors due to overconfidence.

TODAY'S TRUTH

"Therefore, dear friends, since you have been forewarned, be on your guard so that you may not be carried away by the error of the lawless and fall from your secure position." — **2 Peter 3:17**

TODAY'S ACTION STEP

Listen to a podcast.

It doesn't have to be Christian. Listen to anything that you find interesting. Learning about something else will allow your mind to focus on other things than your temptations.

DAY 30

"It is best to avoid the beginnings of evil."
— **Henry David Thoreau**

ENEMY TACTICS

Write down any enemy tactics or temptations you have faced recently. The more you study your enemy, the more you will recognize patterns in your enemy's warfare. The more you learn, the more prepared you will become and the more daily wins you will experience.

I'VE BEEN TEMPTED IN THE FOLLOWING WAYS IN THE LAST 24 HOURS:

____

____

____

THE FOLLOWING PEOPLE/PLACES/THINGS LEAD TO TEMPTING SITUATIONS:

____

____

____

ONE THING I CAN DO BASED ON WHAT I HAVE OBSERVED IS:

____

____

____

ABSTAIN FROM EVIL

Truth be told, lust is just one type of sin that can get the best of you. There are many other ways to get off track. It just happens to be that lust is one of the most common, yet most hidden sins that people face.

As you continue to flush lust from your life, you may also begin to notice wins in battles that are completely unrelated. Do your best to avoid every type of sin, not just sexual sin.

In the same way that an infection can negatively impact many organs in the body, if one infected part of the body begins to regain health, the rest of the body will also begin to regain health.

What other areas of your life seem to be going better now that you've had some success in this area?

TODAY'S TRUTH

"Stay away from every kind of evil."
— 1 Thessalonians 5:22 (NLT)

TODAY'S ACTION STEP

Build a hot fudge sundae.

If you happen to live near a Handel's Homemade Ice Cream and Yogurt shop, go try the "Oree Dough" ice cream flavor. #BestIceCreamEver

Most people don't celebrate enough in life, and you're one day from completing the 31 Day Challenge. That's worth celebrating!

Get those ice cream supplies ready, because you're about to celebrate!

DAY 31

"I am not going to Heaven because I have preached to great crowds or read the Bible many times. I'm going to Heaven just like the thief on the cross who said in that last moment: 'Lord, remember me.'"
— Billy Graham

ENEMY TACTICS

Write down any enemy tactics or temptations you have faced recently. The more you study your enemy, the more you will recognize patterns in your enemy's warfare. The more you learn, the more prepared you will become and the more daily wins you will experience.

I'VE BEEN TEMPTED IN THE FOLLOWING WAYS IN THE LAST 24 HOURS:

____

____

____

THE FOLLOWING PEOPLE/PLACES/THINGS LEAD TO TEMPTING SITUATIONS:

____

____

____

ONE THING I CAN DO BASED ON WHAT I HAVE OBSERVED IS:

____

____

____

HIDE THE WORD

If you have successfully completed all 31 days in a row, then a job well done! Take time to celebrate today… not by sinning, of course!

If you failed in the middle of this challenge, then keep your streak alive and start back over at Day 1 until you have completed 31 days in a row.

The more truth you add to your heart and mind, the greater likelihood of success as you fight this war.

Go back through this guide and see if any verses stand out to you. Write them down somewhere. Take a picture. Print them off. Make a verse the background on your phone. Read a verse 10 times and then try to state it from memory.

The goal is not to check the box that you're being a "good Christian" because you're memorizing scripture. The goal is that you're constantly refreshing your mind with the truth so that when lies present themselves and pick a fight, you won't need to pull out your Bible in order to engage them in the battle.

Choose a verse that has meaning to you and do yourself a favor by memorizing it. Should you choose to do so, I can pretty much guarantee that the next time you're facing a temptation, you'll think of that verse.

I'm sure you're already aware of this, but I want to remind you that even if you have completed this 31 Day Challenge, the war is still waging.

Every day will continue to be a challenge, but now you have tools, momentum, and tactics to get you through even the toughest temptations.

Remember Paul's warning[31] as you move forward:

"[I]f you think you are standing firm, be careful that you don't fall!"

You might even start at the beginning of this book all over again so you're proactively and intentionally fighting this battle every day. Remember that the latest research suggests that new habits are truly solidified after 66 days. Keep this new and healthy trend going in your life.

God's ways are better than our own, and I'm confident you will be thankful should you choose God's ways over selfishness.

Don't give up fighting. Never give up.

TODAY'S TRUTH

"I have hidden your word in my heart that I might not sin against you." — **Psalm 119:11**

TODAY'S ACTION STEP

Memorize a Bible verse.

Throughout the course of the last 31 days, you have been presented with 31 different scriptures. Go back through each day and choose the one that is most impactful, helpful or meaningful to you.

Write it down, put it in the notes section of your phone, make a graphic of it, print it off and tape it to your mirror… do whatever you can to place this verse in front of you so you can naturally learn it.

Once you put this guide down, there's the likelihood that you never pick it up ever again. While that's the natural course of most books, it doesn't have to be the case with scripture.

By memorizing a meaningful verse, you take that verse everywhere you go. The next time you're faced with a temptation, you'll be able to fight that temptation with God's Word planted in your heart.

If no verses stand out to you, consider memorizing the words of Paul that we read on Day 5:

"No temptation has overtaken you except what is common to mankind. And God is faithful; he will not let you be tempted beyond what you can bear. But when you are tempted, he will also provide a way out so that you can endure it." — **1 Corinthians 10:13**

CONGRATS!
YOU REACHED YOUR
LAST MILESTONE!
GREAT JOB!

YOU
CAN
ENDURE

TOUGH QUESTIONS

The following list of questions is intended for you to ask other guys. When you plan to ask them questions, not only does it hold them accountable, but it holds you accountable as well. Don't expect to ask these questions without getting them asked of you in return.

1. When was the last time you looked at porn?

2. What tools or action steps are working for you to avoid lustful situations?

3. Have you done anything since the last time we spoke you shouldn't have done?

4. What is causing you stress or anxiety right now?

5. What question are you hoping I don't ask you right now?

6. Have you lied to me in any of your answers today?

7. How can I pray for you right now?

8. When and where are we meeting next?

LOCATION: _________________ DATE: ___/____

LOCATION: _________________ DATE: ___/____

LOCATION: _________________ DATE: ___/____

LOCATION: _________________ DATE: ___/____

LOCATION: _________________ DATE: ___/____

LOCATION: _________________ DATE: ___/____

LOCATION: _________________ DATE: ___/____

LOCATION: _________________ DATE: ___/____

LOCATION: _________________ DATE: ___/____

LOCATION: _________________ DATE: ___/____

LOCATION: _________________ DATE: ___/____

LOCATION: _________________ DATE: ___/____

ACTION STEPS OVERVIEW

Feel free to utilize any of the daily Action Steps whenever you like to help you push through the Danger Zone of a temptation. Each of the following Action Steps is explained in greater detail on that day's page within this book.

Day 1:   Turn your phone into a weapon.

Day 2:   Protect yourself online.

Day 3:   Invite a few friends over to hang.

Day 4:   Make the big ask.

Day 5:   Start a new project or hobby.

Day 6:   Take a cold shower.

Day 7:   Lift weights.

Day 8:   Move your furniture around.

Day 9:   Go on a run.

Day 10:   Cook a meal.

Day 11:   Listen to a sermon.

Day 12:   Read a book.

Day 13:   Take a prayer walk.

Day 14:   Watch a movie.

Day 15:   Worship.

Day 16:   Write a thank you card.

Day 17:   Text an accountability partner.

Day 18:   Go to the gym.

Day 19:   Check your tire pressure.

Day 20:   Call a friend.

Day 21:   Create a playlist.

Day 22:   Clean out your closet.

Day 23:   Do 30 burpees.

Day 24:   Fix something.

Day 25:   Sharpen your leadership skills.

Day 26:   Donate blood.

Day 27:   Floss.

Day 28:   Wash your car.

Day 29:   Listen to a podcast.

Day 30:   Build a hot fudge sundae.

Day 31:   Memorize a Bible verse.

DEAR SEX TRAFFICKING VICTIM…

I am so, so sorry.

I am so sorry that I ever contributed to the industry that has stolen so much from you. Please forgive me.

I don't know if you had a choice to get into the sex trafficking industry or if you were forced or coerced to join.

Whether it was your choice or not—I am so sorry for the lies you have been told.

You have been told that your value is based on how much money your body can make and how many people you can please.

Your value is much greater than how much money you can make. Your value is much more than what you can offer. You are valuable because you are beautifully and wonderfully made[32]. You have purpose. You have strengths. You have talents. You are more than a paycheck. You are not property to be owned.

If you made the choice to enter this industry on your own as a legal adult, then maybe you were promised more money than you'd know how to spend. Or maybe you were promised drugs, a place to stay, clothes, food, companionship, or something else.

Despite the promises, based on the fact that you're reading this right now, I'm guessing this industry isn't all its cracked up to be.

No matter where you've been or what you've done, I believe two things about you:

1.   God has a plan for your life, and
2.   God's not done with you yet.

As long as you're still alive, God can still use you. He wants to use you. There is no better version of you… than you.

God loves you. He cherishes you. You are His masterpiece.

Don't doubt it. Don't deny it. Choose to believe it.

You still have hope. Freedom is possible. You can get out.

Every single day, men and women, boys and girls just like you escape from the powerful grip of this industry.

You can too.

If you or someone you know needs help, call the National Human Trafficking Hotline, 24 hours a day, 7 days a week at (888) 373-7888 to speak with a specially trained Anti-Trafficking Hotline Advocate. Support is provided in more than 200 languages.

You may text the National Human Trafficking Hotline at 233733.

DEAR SEX TRAFFICKER…

The harm you are causing is indescribable.

If you are filming; producing or creating porn; running an escort service; operating a massage parlor; recruiting cam models; selling sex slaves or exchanging anything of value in exchange for sexual actions—you are ruining lives.

It doesn't matter how much money you make or have been promised—you are ruining lives.

Please stop believing the lies—you are ruining lives.

If there is anyone on this planet who you actually care about, think about what it would be like if his or her life were to be ruined.

There are other ways to make a living. There are honorable ways to make money. You don't have to continue to contribute to such a despicable and disgusting industry.

Please consider a different career.

There are plenty of career options that take advantage of all the positive attributes you have that help build, inspire and motivate people rather than tear down, destroy and manipulate people.

What you have to contribute to mankind is much more than what you are currently offering.

If you have no idea how to find another career, please accept my free gift to you: *The Secret to Success*. It is an ebook that will help you identify potential careers that will allow you to earn a living based on honorable talents and abilities you have.

Download my free ebook at mattmizell.com/success.

If you continue doing what you have been doing, you will continue to ruin lives.

Please stop.

ABOUT THE AUTHOR

School got out early every Wednesday when I was in mid school. One day in the 7th grade, I got dropped off by the bus after a half a day at school and one of my friends offered for me to come over and check out this "cool magazine".

That "cool magazine" was the first Playboy I ever saw.

Decades later, I can still remember vivid images I saw that afternoon.

Unfortunately, that magazine unleashed a craving and desire for me, and what started innocently enough on a Wednesday afternoon turned into a full addition and struggle with porn that would last for years.

After dealing with my addiction for nearly a decade, I finally got sick and tired of the feeling of disgust and disappointment in myself and made the choice to quit cold turkey.

I failed. I tried again, and failed again.

But the third time I tried, I finally saw success.

Since that third attempt, there have been a few relapses in the years after where I clicked on the wrong image from the wrong site and found myself spiraling down the dangerous and slippery slope of porn.

In each of those instances, I confessed my sin quickly to guys who want the best for me, and thankfully I have been able to consistently avoid the traps that surround me on a daily basis.

The more guys I meet, the more guys I discover currently are drowning in guilt and shame and feel as though there's no way out.

There is a way out, if you choose to find it and take it. I'm living proof.

I am now a pastor and live in Farmington, New Mexico with my wife and three kids.

Connect with me at mattmizell.com.

ACKNOWLEDGEMENTS

A special thanks to the following people for providing feedback, support and critique for this project:

Ashten Mizell

Chase Feindel

Jeff Brady

Colton Wheeler

Eric West

Joe Palmer

Steven Murphy

Keenan Klamer

Steve Schick

Shea Cullen

Doug Clark

Adam Kuntz

Steven Ballard

Scott Stratchan

Jeff Myers

Ryan Greenwald

Jason Greenwald

Nicholas Marsden

Chad Gothmann

NOTES

[1] PMO Definition
https://www.urbandictionary.com/define.php?term=PMO
Accessed on 12/29/17

[2] The Silence Breakers
http://time.com/time-person-of-the-year-2017-silence-breakers
Accessed on 12/29/17

[3] Fallen Powerful Men
https://www.nbcnews.com/storyline/sexual-misconduct/weinstein-here-s-growing-list-men-accused-sexual-misconduct-n816546
Accessed on 12/29/17

[4] Sex Trafficking Definition
https://uaht.org/wp-content/uploads/sex-trafficking.jpg
Accessed on 01/14/18

[5] Traffic Victims Protections Act
https://www.state.gov/j/tip/laws
Accessed on 01/16/18

[6] Sex Trafficking Revenue
https://www.urban.org/sites/default/files/alfresco/publication-pdfs/413047-Estimating-the-Size-and-Structure-of-the-Underground-Commercial-Sex-Economy-in-Eight-Major-US-Cities.PDF
Accessed on 01/16/18

[7] Porn Fueling Sex Trafficking
https://www.wearethorn.org/wp-content/uploads/2015/02/Survivor_Survey_r5.pdf
Accessed on 01/18/18

[8] Sex Trade Age Statistics
https://www.dosomething.org/us/facts/11-facts-about-human-trafficking
Accessed on 01/16/18

[9] 1 Corinthians 6:18

[10] Length of Time to Make New Habits
https://jamesclear.com/new-habit
Accessed on 01/18/18

[11] 1 Samuel 17

[12] Self-Harm Antidote
https://www.calmclinic.com/anxiety/self-harm
Accessed on 01/18/18

[13] HabitBull® Premium Habit Tracker is a registered trademark of HabitBull. This publication does not imply any endorsement or partnership with HabitBull. For more information, visit www.habitbull.com.

[14] James 1:22

[15] http://www.covenanteyes.com

[16] https://chrome.google.com/webstore/detail/safe-browser

[17] https://x3watch.com

[18] http://www1.k9webprotection.com

[19] http://www.rtribe.org

[20] CS Lewis, *The Four Loves* (1960)

[21] Cold Shower
https://www.artofmanliness.com/2010/01/18/the-james-bond-shower-a-shot-of-cold-water-for-health-and-vitality
Accessed on 01/18/18

[22] Genesis 1:1

[23] Acts 16:16-40

[24] Matthew 5:37 (HCSB)

[25] Ecclesiastes 5:5

[26] Routine Habits
http://journals.sagepub.com/doi/10.1177/0146167209360665
Accessed on 01/18/18

[27] Exercise For Stress & Anxiety
https://adaa.org/living-with-anxiety/managing-anxiety/exercise-stress-and-anxiety
Accessed on 01/18/18

[28] Dr. James C. Dobson, *Love Must Be Tough* (1983)

[29] Professional Sports Annual Revenue
https://www.marketwatch.com/story/the-nfl-made-13-billion-last-season-see-how-it-stacks-up-against-other-leagues-2016-07-01
Accessed on 02/16/2018

[30] Porn Annual Revenue
https://www.nbcnews.com/business/business-news/things-are-looking-americas-porn-industry-n289431
Accessed on 02/16/2018

[31] 1 Corinthians 10:12

[32] Psalm 139:14 (KJV)

WARNING SIGNS OF
CHILD SEX TRAFFICKING

WARNING SIGNS THAT AN INDIVIDUAL IS BEING TRAFFICKED:

- Signs of physical abuse such as burn marks, bruises or cuts
- Unexplained absences from school, truancy
- Less appropriately dressed than before
- Sexualized behavior
- Overly tired or falls asleep in class
- Withdrawn, depressed, or distracted
- Brags about making or having lots of money
- Displays expensive clothes, accessories, or shoes
- New tattoo (tattoos are often used by pimps as a way to brand victims.)
- Older boyfriend, new friends with a different lifestyle, or gang involvement
- Disjointed family connections, running away, living with friends, or experiencing homelessness

PIMPS/TRAFFICKERS OFTEN EXHIBIT THE FOLLOWING BEHAVIORS OR CHARACTERISTICS:

- Jealous, controlling and violent
- Significantly older than female companions
- Promise things that seem too good to be true
- Encourage victims to engage in illegal activities to achieve their goals and dreams
- Buys expensive gifts or owns expensive items
- Is vague about his/her profession
- Pushy or demanding about sex
- Encourages inappropriate sexual behavior
- Makes the victim feel responsible for his/her financial stability. Very open about financial matters.

TO REPORT A TIP OR CONNECT WITH ANTI-TRAFFICKING SERVICES IN YOUR AREA, CONTACT:

U.S. Immigration and Customs Enforcement

1-866-347-2423 (U.S. & Canada)
1-802-872-6199 (International Calls)

ICE's hotline to report suspected child predators and any suspicious activity.
Call or complete an online tip form.

National Human Trafficking Hotline

1-888-373-7888

The National Human Trafficking Hotline is a national, toll-free hotline, available to answer calls from anywhere in the country, 24 hours a day, 7 days a week, every day of the year.

National Center for Missing & Exploited Children

1-800-843-5678

If you have information about a missing child or suspected child sexual exploitation, call to report it or visit their website, www.missingkids.com/cybertipline.com.

The National Runaway Safeline

1-800-RUNAWAY

The National Runaway Switchboard serves as the federally-designated national communication system for homeless and runaway youth. Through hotline and online services, NRS provides crisis intervention, referrals to local resources, and education and prevention services to youth, families and community members throughout the country 24 hours a day, 365 days a year.

4 ways to take action against domestic minor sex trafficking

Write a letter to your local media editor or congressional representative, to inform them about domestic minor trafficking. Let your representatives and newspapers know that victims of child sex trafficking exist in every state, even your own. Ask your legislators to commit to providing safe shelters for victims, and increased penalties for buyers and traffickers. The more phone calls, letters, and emails your legislator receives, the more action will occur. Visit our "Join the Cause" page for more information.

Host or attend an awareness event in your community! How? Host an awareness event, sports competition, fundraiser, candlelight vigil, march, movie screening, dinner, walk, run, yoga or Zumba class with free materials and information provided by Shared Hope International. Who's in charge? You are! Gather your friends, neighbors and colleagues. We'll also connect you with other Shared Hope supporters in your area. Together, we can make a difference!

Fight for justice online! Use social media and blogs to spread the word to your online community of friends, family and neighbors. Participate and invite your friends to our Facebook or Twitter accounts. Spread awareness by sharing videos, blogs, articles, pictures and other information via social media. Join the conversation on YouTube, Vimeo, Twitter or Facebook (for both the Defenders and Shared Hope).

Join the cause! Become an Ambassador of Hope or a Defender. Ambassadors of Hope go through an online or in-person training to become equipped to speak on behalf of Shared Hope International. Defenders are men who take a pledge and take action to fight against domestic minor sex trafficking and the commercial sex industry. Visit **www.theDefendersUSA.org** for more information.

Shared Hope International • Vancouver, WA • 360-693-8100 • 1-866-HER-LIFE • Fax: 360-695-9489
Shared Hope International • Washington, DC • 703-351-8062 • Fax: 703-351-8064 • www.sharedhope.org

Learn to help those who are suicidal
by downloading Matt's free ebook,

THIRTEEN REASONS WHY NOT
A Step-By-Step Guide to Helping Depressed & Suicidal Teenagers.

Download at 13reasonswhynot.com.
Also available in print at Amazon.com.

Learn how to achieve true success in Matt's book,

THE SECRET TO SUCCESS
3 Steps to Unlocking Your True Potential.

Download for free at www.mattmizell.com/success.

Build a legacy and become a
better leader at www.mattmizell.com.

#leaderworthfollowing